transformed by the spirit

For Zilene Don't Give up
Jesus Loves You.
Juan Cubero

the story of juan cubero as told to dennis smith

Printed in the USA

Unless otherwise noted all Scripture quotations are taken from the Holy Bible, King James Version.

Cover designed by David Berthiaume
Text designed by Greg Solie • AltamontGraphics.com

ISBN: 978-0-9815736-6-3

Table of Contents

Introduction

The story you are about to read is the true story of Juan Cubero, who I learned to know shortly after he became a Christian. The young man I met was very different from the former young man who had been deeply involved in drugs and gangs.

As I came to know Juan and learn of his story I felt impressed to help him write his testimony of how the Lord led him from serving Satan to being a minister for God; from dealing drugs to sharing the gospel of Jesus Christ.

I am always amazed to see how the grace of God can change one's life so dramatically. Such was the change in Juan's life. I have seen the Lord use the talents this young man previously used in the service of the enemy of God to now serve his Lord and Master, Jesus Christ. I know you also will be amazed to see the grace of God working in Juan's life.

Since I first met Juan several years ago, the Lord has called him to share his testimony to young and old nationally and internationally, on radio, TV and live audiences. The messages the Lord has put on his heart to share have been used by God to draw hundreds of young men and women to Jesus Christ either for the first time or to renew their relationship with Jesus.

Juan's and my prayer is that all who read this book will have their faith reaffirmed in a loving God, who does not give up on His children, even when from a human point of view all looks hopeless. Juan knows that God hears and answers a mother's prayers. Our desire is that this book can be used by God to save even one young person from entering Satan's snare of drugs, immorality and ill-gotten money.

As you read Juan's story you will see that God's loving grace can change the hardest heart and reach to the deepest depths of sin. If you are in a situation that seems hopeless, this book will give you hope. If you feel the gospel of Jesus Christ is just a religious theory or pious story, you will find a gospel that can save even the vilest of sinners. If you desire genuine peace and happiness, you will find the source of true happiness as you read Juan's story.

May God bless you as you read of His grace revealed in the life of Juan Cubero.

Pastor Dennis Smith
New Haven, CT

CHAPTER ONE

How It All Began

The time in my life that you are about to read is not a time that I am proud of. I made many wrong decisions, which led to great tragedies in my life. There were many people that I hurt and I am very sorry for my past sinful actions. I have often wished that I could go back in time and make things right. I thank my Lord that He is a forgiving God whose grace is greater than all my sin.

Satan has a way of making some very wrong activities look attractive at first. However, any time we choose to follow his ways and turn from God's ways we will suffer great loss and pain. We will end up hurting others and ourselves.

I hesitate to share the following description of my former life before I accepted Christ as my Savior. As Pastor Smith writes it, I pray that all I describe God will use as a warning "not to go there" to any reader who is beginning to enter such a life-style or is currently caught up in a life of crime. My story clearly reveals that God's grace can change the life of anyone who chooses to turn to Christ. So, if you are reading this booklet because you want to change your life and find real peace and happiness, I can verify that God is with you to enable you to escape the web of Satan and find real happiness in Christ.

I was born January 11, 1974 in New Haven, Connecticut. When I was four years old my mother and father divorced, and I stayed with my mother. In 1984 we moved to Puerto Rico. We located in a poor neighborhood, Nuestra Senora de Covadonga Public Housing Development, which is known for its high rate of criminal activities. Drug dealing and usage, illegal weapons and murders were commonplace. My father was living in Florida so I had no contact with him for many years.

Covadonga Public Housing—Puerto Rico

A child, learns from what he sees. I saw that if someone killed a person the killer got great respect from others. The more violent one was the more women were attracted to him and he ran the project. It became clear to me that drug dealers made lots of money and were able to buy whatever they wanted. They had what appeared to be the "good life." I was to learn how truly wrong my conclusions were.

My neighborhood was very violent. The drug dealers and gangs ran the neighborhood. At times the police tried to gain control, and would come and have shoot-outs with the gangs. It was not unusual for innocent people to get shot and killed. Stray bullets would fly into the apartments and hit the occupants. Many times my family and I would have to sleep in the hallway at night in order to be protected from the stray bullets.

I saw numerous murders by the time I reached my teen years. Once I saw a friend killed by his assailant putting 94 bullets in him. On another occasion a couple friends and I were sitting on some stair railings in the neighborhood. We saw a black car quietly drive up behind a nearby building. A drug dealer was not far from us. The men got out of the black car and began shooting at us. As we ran, I could hear the bullets flying past my ears, and sparking off the road and concrete walls of the buildings. We were being shot at with AK-47s. As we ran the shooters then turned their weapons on the drug dealer, who had been standing near us. He was shot to death.

In my neighborhood the drug dealers outgunned the police. They had AK-47s, M-16s, grenades, bazookas, bulletproof vests; all of which had been stolen from the National Guard. Life where I grew up was truly survival of the toughest and most violent persons. After all, that was how one got respect, which was often one's protection as well.

When I was in prison a friend told me that he and his boys had planned to kill an individual one night. After he said that I realized that was the very night I and a couple others were riding in the car with the man they planned to kill. They became aware that I and others were with him in the car. So they decided not to attack him that night. If they had come after him, I would have been killed also. Later they did kill him. This is how car massacres happen.

As I got older I wanted to prove my self, and show my friends that I was tough and not afraid of anything. Store theft and other minor criminal activity were commonplace. On several occasions I was involved in pistol-whipping someone for drug money they owed, drug shoot-outs, beating individuals in order to make a point that I was not someone to be "messed" with. I was continually trying to prove myself and get respect from others.

Peer pressure is a primary reason that many youth get into trouble by using drugs, alcohol, getting into fights and other criminal activity. Young people do these things to be accepted by their friends and become a part of the group. I made this mistake on many occasions in my past. Many of my friends are dead today because of this pressure to do things to be accepted that finally led to their death.

Juan (left) and his boys in a Puerto Rican parade

This was the reason I began using weed, coke, etc. I thought these things proved I was a man. The sad truth is these very things will make us less of a man, and can ultimately lead to poor health, financial poverty and even death. Instead of becoming a young man who can better himself and provide for his family, these things lead many young men to be incapable of meeting their own needs or their family's needs if they have a family.

How It All Began

After becoming a Christian I now realize that we don't have to prove anything to anyone. Why is that? When we know God loves and accepts us we know we are approved by the great God of the universe. There is no one greater or more important than God. So, once we know we have His approval by accepting His Son, Jesus, as our Savior we have peace in our heart.

> "Therefore being justified by faith, we have peace with God through our Lord Jesus Christ" Romans 5:1

There is no peace like the peace we can have with God. If you don't have peace in your heart I invite you to make the decision to give your life to God. I can tell you from personal experience you will never regret that decision.

Recently I went to my old neighborhood in Puerto Rico. I discovered that many of my old friends were either in prison or dead. I also found that the next generation of youth was now running the projects. They were the ones now involved in drug trafficking and other violence. It hurt me to see the needle marks in their arms. Their physical appearance was deteriorating because of the drugs. These activities were destroying their lives.

Satan is especially attacking you and me. He wants to destroy the youth because he knows the powerful work they can do and influence they can have. God knows this also. For He tells us:

> "And it shall come to pass afterward, that I will pour out my spirit upon all flesh; and your sons and your daughters shall prophesy, your old men shall dream dreams, your young men shall see visions." Joel 2:28

Satan knows God's plan for young people, so he tries to keep this from happening. He uses drugs, immoral sexual relationships, crime, and gangs, to keep this from happening in our lives. God's plan will always come to pass. In the Bible we read of many young men who God used to do mighty things for Him. The Bible tells us:

> "Let no man despise thy youth; but be thou an example of the believers, in word, in conversation, in charity, in spirit, in faith, in purity." 1 Timothy 4:12

The Bible tells us of the young man David, who God used in many mighty ways. When he was still a young man God used him to defeat Israel's enemies by slaying the giant Goliath. Joseph was about 16 years old when he was sold as a slave in Egypt. God used this young man to ultimately be a savior to the nation of Egypt from a terrible famine and even save his family at that time. Some of the disciples Jesus chose to follow Him and establish his church were young men. Throughout the history of God's people and church young men and women have been used by God to do mighty things for Him.

So, if you want to see God do mighty things through you; if you want to see God do miracles, I challenge you to give your life to the Lord today. You will be amazed at what He can do for and through you.

There is nothing wrong with being different. The Bible tells us:

> "Wherefore come out from among them, and be ye separate, saith the Lord, and touch not the unclean thing; and I will receive you, And will be a Father unto you, and ye shall be my sons and daughters, saith the Lord Almighty." 2 Corinthians 6:17, 18

Christians will be different from the world; different from their non-Christian friends. They will listen to different music and participate in different activities. Christians will stand out in a crowd. They will be healthier physically, emotionally and spiritually. They will see God's mighty works. Jesus said

How It All Began

"Ye are the salt of the earth." Matthew 5:13

Salt gives life, creates thirst, melts ice, and gives flavor. The Christian is to do these things. We are to; bring the life of God to others, be used by God to create a thirst for Him, give flavor (joy) to life and melt icy cold relationships.

To be this salt the Christian will be unlike their worldly friends. The Bible tells us the story of Daniel and his three friends. They chose to be different from all around them. They chose to follow God's counsel concerning what to eat and drink. The result was that they were healthier and smarter than the others. Daniel chose to pray as usual when a law was passed not to pray to anyone but the king. As a result he was thrown into the lion's den. Daniel saw a miracle that night by God keeping the lions from attacking and killing him. Daniel's three friends chose to be different and not bow down to the king's image. Because of their choice they were thrown into a hot burning furnace. The result of their choice to be different is that they saw God work a miracle in their behalf and the fire did not touch them; they did not even smell of smoke. So, choose to be different for God and you will see miracles.

The Bible tells us that Satan is the God of this world and that the majority are blinded by him.

> "In whom the god of this world hath blinded the minds of them which believe not, lest the light of the glorious gospel of Christ, who is the image of God, should shine unto them." 2 Corinthians 4:4

It is important to be like Daniel and his friends and not worship the god of this world by following the ways and pleasures of this world. It is vital that we be willing to be different from the crowd and follow God.

I decided to leave school in 1988 and spend a vacation with my father, in order to get to know him better. This ended my formal education at the eighth grade. Being filled with anger, I had many confrontations with my father and his wife. He wanted to change my life for the better. However, I was very rebellious. How much better it would have been for me if I had listened to him at that time. However, I thought I knew what was best for me. So instead of taking his advice I did just the opposite. I met some friends in the area who were into stealing cars. I joined them in this activity. I went so far as trying to steal my father's car. He caught me trying to steal it, and decided He couldn't handle me any longer. I don't hold this decision against him. He tried to help me, but I was too foolish to listen. So after nine months I returned to Puerto Rico to live with my mother again.

When I returned I had no motivation to work at a steady job. I found my old friends and saw that they were making money, and had everything they wanted without working for it. To me it looked like they had the right idea. So I started joining them in drug dealing. First it was selling marijuana, which led to crack cocaine and heroine. Of course, the latter two drugs made me much more money. As time passed I moved up the ladder in the drug organization. My success as a dealer moved me up to the table where they made the drugs. This brought me much more money and respect, which was my ultimate goal. Making money, getting respect, making connections with other drug dealers began to bring me the material things I wanted. But what a heavy price one pays who enters the dark, violent world of drugs.

I began getting organized with other drug dealers in other projects and around the island. This way I could move more drugs and make more money. I became known and respected more and more in the drug world. Even though I was making more money I was still only a lower level "hustler." My goal was to become a "kingpin," who was someone that was high up in the drug organization making 50, 60, 70 thousand dollars or more a day.

My success and reputation as a "hustler" earned me the trust I needed with the "kingpins" in the drug business. They began giving me more money and more drugs. I became their middle man receiving many kilos of cocaine from them to distribute to Boston and New York City. When distributed I brought many hundreds of thousands of dollars back to them. Their trust in me continued to grow. I became one of their most successful middle men. I knew how to dress, act and carry myself not looking like a drug dealer. Hence, I was able to make many drug carrying trips from Puerto Rico to the East coast without being profiled and arrested.

I thought I was well on my way to "success and riches," not knowing that if I continued in the path I was traveling I would either be killed or kill someone, and spend the rest of my life in prison.

Now as I reflect on my past I realize and see how God has changed my life from a negative to a positive experience. I never realized how destructive my life was to others and myself. My involvement in the drug trade was actually destroying the lives of those who took the very drugs that were making me successful in the business. I was becoming a success by destroying others.

CHAPTER TWO

Busted!

On the afternoon of January 26, 1993, I and two others arrived at Logan International Airport in Boston, Massachusetts, from Puerto Rico. Each of us was carrying a bag containing significant amounts of cocaine. We had met three girls on the plane. They were walking behind us as we made our way through the airport. We occasionally looked around to talk with the girls. We finally made our way out of the airport and onto the sidewalk.

Then a man approached behind us and pulled credentials from his pocket. He identified himself as a DEA federal narcotics agent. He had observed our looking around to speak to the girls and he thought we were nervous, looking to see if we were being followed. This was in God's divine province. Immediately I told my two friends to split and we began walking in opposite directions. The agent then called to me, "What's going on? Where are they going?"

I said nothing in reply. My two friends were still nearby. So I told them to stop. We looked at one another in dread of what might happen next. The narcotics agent asked if he could ask us some questions. I said, "Yeah."

He asked me why we had traveled to Boston. I replied that we had come to visit friends. He then asked us for identification and our airline tickets. I stated that I had lost mine. My two friends gave him theirs. The agent noticed that the tickets were one way tickets from San Juan to Boston, and had been paid for in cash. He then returned the two tickets and other identification items to us.

The agent asked us to go back into the terminal. We didn't want to, and I told him that we were waiting for someone to pick us up and we might miss him if we went back inside. The agent insisted, so we went back inside the terminal with him. The agent asked if it was okay for him to question us some more. I agreed. We went to the lower level of the terminal and the agent asked me again why we had traveled to Boston.

I said we came to visit a sick cousin. He then asked me the name of my cousin. Since I made up the story, that question also caught me off guard and I was slow coming up with a name. Then he asked me what the sickness was, and again I didn't know what to say. So I said I didn't know, but maybe she had cancer. Again this hesitation, which caused the agent to be suspicious, was of God's doing. I had transported drugs many times before and knew very well how to conduct myself. This time God overruled; for He had other plans for me.

The agent then asked to look into my bag. I knelt down and opened it up shuffling the contents trying to hide the drugs. He then searched my bag and saw what appeared to be one kilogram of cocaine. He then placed all three of us under arrest. Later a drug detecting dog was directed to determine if there were drugs in the bags of the other two individuals who were with me. The dog indicated there were drugs in their bags also. The next day search warrants were obtained for these other two bags. Cocaine was found in each bag, a kilogram in one and two kilograms in the other. The agent later testified that in his experience with the United States Customs Service, he had observed kilograms of cocaine with similar wrappings and markings, which had been imported into the United States directly from Colombia. The agent was correct. Puerto Rico has become a major distribution center for drugs coming from Colombia to the United States. Boston and New York City are major destinations for these drugs.

Busted!

When I was arrested for drug possession and intent to distribute at Logan International Airport I was angry that I got caught. I knew that prison was not a pleasant place and had no desire to be incarcerated. The authorities threatened me with a 40-year sentence. Then they offered me a deal. They would reduce my sentence if I cooperated with them by leading them to those higher up in the drug organization.

I knew the chances I was taking in my drug transporting activity. I also knew that my family would be in danger if I got caught and became an informer. So I decided to take whatever prison sentence was given me without revealing anyone else as involved. After several court procedures I was finally given a 5-year sentence in a federal penitentiary plus four years probation.

Juan—Federal Prison Lorreto, PA, in 1996

At the time I had no idea that God was using this event that seemed so terrible to me to actually save my life. My past had been filled with violence. At the time of the writing of this booklet, in the category of violent crime, Puerto Rico ranks second in the United States and her territories, and sixth worldwide. I know now that if God hadn't so dramatically pulled me out of my life of crime I too would have been killed. The reason I am telling my story is because most of my past friends who were involved with me in the drug business are dead, murdered, and killed in shoot-outs with other drug dealers and the police. Instead, God had other plans for me. I thank Him for patiently working in my life and overruling many events.

CHAPTER THREE

Prison Life

Life in a prison is not a pleasant experience. I never thought I would get caught. When I was in prison I had no understanding of God's leading in my life. I was frustrated that I could not be free, doing whatever I wanted and making money. Now I was enclosed in four walls and being totally controlled in my every activity.

The first year was the most difficult. During that time my brother was killed in the projects in Puerto Rico. I was frustrated since I could do nothing to revenge his murder. However, I did make plans about how I would take revenge for his death when I got out. Little did I know that the Lord would overrule these plans, which I thank Him for today.

As I grew up I saw very clearly that men don't cry. It was a sign of weakness. If any of my friends would have seen me cry they would have looked down on me, and I would have lost their respect. When in prison I at times felt overwhelmed being enclosed in the four walls, controlled, unable to make my own decisions, and separated from love ones on special occasions. It seemed that I meant nothing to anyone. Now I seemed deserted and alone. My drug business friends didn't care if I lived or died. The very ones who had looked up to me and given me respect could care less about me now.

At times I felt so overwhelmed that I would fall on my face in tears in my cell and cry out to God; "Why is this happening to me? Why do I have to go through this? What have I done?" How ignorant I was. I actually thought I had done nothing wrong. Drug dealing was a way life, and the killings were justified in my mind. I was in such a state of confusion. I truly didn't know right from wrong. I didn't realize it, but I desperately needed God in my life in order for me to know the true meaning of life and how to achieve real happiness. All my values had been wrong due to the environment I had grown up in and I didn't know it. I know that many others are in that same situation right now. They think they are on the right path for real success and happiness, not knowing that they are headed for destruction. How true the Bible verse that says, "There is a way which seemeth right unto a man, but the end thereof are the ways of death" (Proverbs 14:12).

Juan in the prison yard at Federal Prison, Fairton, NJ 1994

I was the kind of person who would come to God briefly when I was in trouble. For the first year in prison I was under great stress and felt in great danger. This experience caused me to give my life to the Lord one day when attending a Christian group who would come to the prison twice weekly. That gave me peace for a while. When the pressure was off due to the peace God had given me I began feeling prison was okay for me and I adjusted to prison life. So I foolishly began drifting away from God. I knew I was getting farther and farther from God, but I continued to neglect the Spirit's promptings to come back. The next thing I knew I was becoming involved in the prison gangs, and I was back to my old value system of power and respect.

I was sentenced for five years. I spent the first year in a prison in Boston. Then they transferred me to Danbury, Connecticut. After that, I was transferred to Lewisburg, Pennsylvania, prison which is also called "the big house." Finally, I was taken to the Federal Correctional Institution (FCI) in Fairton, New Jersey. I spent three years in this facility.

During my stay in Fairton I went back into my old lifestyle-attitude problems, taking drugs, selling contraband, fighting to get respect. I became a leader in a gang called Neta, which originated in 1980 in penitentiaries in Puerto Rico. The Netas along with the Latin Kings ran the gang world in the prison. The Latin Kings were considered "cousins" to the Netas because both are Latin gangs. These two gangs made up the largest population in the prison. In other prisons the largest population might be the "Black Muslins," "Crypts," "Bloods," or "White Supremacist." Whoever had the largest group ran the prison from inside.

We would often have meetings to discuss plans for keeping our power and control of the prison from the inside. On occasion we would be given a contract by a minority ethnic group in the prison asking us to do them a favor. For instance, perhaps an Italian group wanted some other prisoner out of the prison because they knew he was an informant. They would put out a contract on this individual asking us to hurt him badly.

Whenever an individual is "stabbed" the prison administration will move him to another facility fearing that if he stayed he would be killed. At other times contracts were even made to kill another prisoner. Our gang was always paid well in money or drugs to carry out these contracts. Now I see how evil and destructive such values and activities are. It would have been so much better for me if I only I had stayed with the Lord.

Weapons were handmade and always available in the prison. Some of the weapons were shanks (knives), swords, shank proof vests, small mouth blades, hand blades tied to the wrist, and blades in the hair. Some prisoners would carry a weapon constantly. When someone doesn't know the Lord he feels alone and vulnerable. If I would have known the Lord at that time I would have realized He was my protector and I had nothing to fear.

I say this because there are prisoners who are Christian. Even though they are in prison they are free. I saw men living in the most dangerous situations maintaining great peace, having no fear. As mentioned before, for a while I attended meetings with a Christian group, and began experiencing the peace of God for myself. However, I still hadn't made a full commitment to the Lord to turn my back on the things of the world. So that caused me to drift away from the Lord after six months, and return to my old life-style and values. This caused me to have many problems in the years that followed. Looking back, how foolish I was to leave what the Lord had led me into, a relationship with Himself that was bringing me peace.

If I had stayed with the Lord my prison experience would have been much better in helping myself and others find the same peace I had found by accepting Jesus Christ as my Savior. But I didn't stay close to the Lord. Instead, thinking I knew best, I allowed my old life-style and values to run my life. I found myself in deeper problems. I thank the Lord for overruling on several occasions, without which could have led to longer imprisonment or even my death.

On one occasion I was confronted by a Muslim prisoner from a different ethnic background than me. He was very large and felt he could do as he pleased in many situations. On many occasions he would enter the TV room where many of us were watching a movie. He would change channels in order to watch what he wanted giving no consideration to the rest in the room. This happened several times. No one said anything to him wanting to avoid any problems.

Such confrontations could lead to a fight and even death. Being controlled by my old false values, I decided to confront him one day. During the argument he tried to intimidate me and said, "What are you going to do about it?" I felt disrespect, which challenged me in front of the other inmates. This was not a good thing to happen since the others would begin disrespecting me also. I had learned this false value growing up in the projects of Puerto Rico; only the strong survive. I believed that turning away from a challenge was cowardly.

As a Christian I have discovered that God gives us a strong sense of self worth and value. The more we come to experience His love for us the stronger our sense of self worth grows. Today I find my value in God and His plans for me. I don't have to prove anything to anyone. Also, before I came to know the Lord, I was filled with anger. Anytime I thought someone was showing me disrespect I felt the anger surface and I was ready to defend my wounded ego.

Now I feel great peace in the Lord. I don't feel the anger as I once did. If someone challenges me today, I may still feel a little surge of anger, but immediately the Lord takes control of me and gives me the strength to turn away. I have found that the Apostle Paul's words apply to every believer in Jesus Christ,

> "I am crucified with Christ: nevertheless I live; yet not I, but Christ liveth in me: and the life which I now live in the flesh I live by the faith of the Son of God, who loved me, and gave himself for me." Galatians 2:20

I find it amazing that when we accept Jesus as our Savior powerful changes happen in us. It is truly as though our "old self" has been crucified with Christ. The old self will still try to control us at times. However, when the Muslim inmate had challenged me I was far from being a Christian. Therefore my old vengeful self took over, and I decided to take matters in my own hands instead of walking away from the situation. This prideful attitude brought me more problems.

I went to the welding shop where I used to work, and got a sharp piece of metal to use as a knife or shank. I knew where my antagonist was. So I hid the shank inside the sleeve of my sweat shirt and approached the man from behind planning to stab him in the back. As I approached him I happened to walk by the window where the prison guards were stationed. They saw me and sensed what I was about to do. So they came out and stopped me. They found the shank and took me and the other man to segregation (the hole). I was charged with attempted assault. I was very angry that I had been caught.

As a result of this incident I was put in isolation for three months where I was let out of the cell for exercise only one hour a day. I was allowed to shower three times a week. I continued to feel this punishment was unjustified. I became more and more angry, especially toward the black Muslims.

Now as I look back, I praise God that He intervened to stop me from harming the man. If I had stabbed him he could have been killed. Also, I would have been imprisoned much longer. I am amazed that the Lord works in our lives even when we are turning our back on Him at the time. He certainly continued to lead and protect me when I was still rebelling against Him. I have come to learn that we have a very loving heavenly Father.

Because of the incident I was transferred to a prison in Pennsylvania called Lorreto, which is also a federal prison. Now I found myself separated from my gang brothers. In fact, the dominant population in this prison was black Muslims. I was filled with rage toward this ethnic group because of what had happened. I literally wanted to strike out at all of them.

Because of this, I decided to get all the Latin brothers together in order to form my own gang. I would meet every bus that arrived with new prisoners and identify myself to all the Latin prisoners. I would give them soap, food, clothes, etc.—things that they would need. This way I began developing friendships, and a Latin gang began to develop. I had learned that a "snitch" cannot be trusted. Therefore, I would always ask to see their papers to see what they were in prison for. These papers would indicate if they had been an informant. These individuals would not be included in the gang.

The Latin gang grew to the point where we could confront the black Muslims if necessary in order to get respect. In time a confrontation happened when the Muslims tried to intimidate one of our gang members in the gym. Word of the incident came to me. I and about 50 other Latins went to the gym and confronted the Muslims. They saw that we had grown in strength and could no longer be intimidated. So their leader talked with me about "squashing" the problem. From that point on I knew there would not be any more incidents like that.

Now as a Christian I look at all men as my brothers whether they are Latin, black, white, etc. The problems I describe above were caused by men, myself included, who felt very insecure and were easily threatened. We all had the same mentality. Now that I have come to know Christ as my Savior I see how foolish all that is. When we personally know God's love for us we come to know that we are of great value to God. In fact, God gave His Son, Jesus, to die for all races no matter what our color or ethnic background. "God so loved the world that He gave his only begotten Son, that whosoever believeth in him should not perish, but have everlasting life" (John 3:16).

I find it amazing to realize that the Bible says "But God commendeth his love toward us, in that, while we were yet sinners, Christ died for us" (Romans 5:8). Now that I look back I wonder how I could have ever wanted to do harm to another person. I have discovered that when we experience God's love for us, we begin loving others as God loves us.

I have also found that the more of God's love I experience the more peace and security I have. As the Bible says, "There is no fear in love; but perfect love casteth out fear: because fear hath torment …" (1 John 4:18). Now my desire is that everyone I knew in prison would come to know God's love for them. I believe such an experience is the best rehabilitation any prisoner could have.

After the confrontation with the black Muslims we felt they were not a threat to us any longer. Therefore, we became very confident of our power and position in the prison. About this time I became aware of a "white" prisoner who had some marijuana. I had been able to smuggle money inside the prison. So I asked one of my gang members, who told me about the marijuana, to offer him $100 for what ever amount of drugs he had. He did what I asked and brought me the marijuana.

My primary motive was to distribute it in the prison, which would give my gang a sense of leadership and the source of drugs in the prison. This would cause the other prisoners to look up to us, and we would be able to get many favors from them. The word spread quickly about my gang being the drug source. This also created a problem because of "snitches" among the prisoners who would inform the prison staff. Therefore, on occasion we would have to shut down the drug sales for a while until things cooled down.

At this time in my life I was using and selling drugs, running the gang feeling I was "the man" having the respect of everyone. Little did I know that I was just fooling myself and leading others toward their eternal destruction. The Bible tells us that "… by one man's disobedience many were made sinners …" (Romans 5:19). This verse certainly describes what I was doing with my life. I was actually working for Satan, being used by him to lead many men to disobedience of God.

My life was anything but a glory to God. Instead, I was serving the enemy of God. How much trouble I would have saved myself if I had been a Christian and lived my life as Paul counsels us. "Whether therefore ye eat, or drink, or whatsoever ye do, do all to the glory of God" (1 Corinthians 10:31). Looking back, how much better it would have been if I had been a Christian during my prison years. Then I could have been used by God to help others come to know God's love for them, and they could have avoided many self-destructive activities and habits.

Now I had reached my last six months in prison. I was looking forward to getting out. A friend who was with me when I set up the gang knew I was to be released soon. So he asked me to support him in becoming the next leader of the "Neta." I agreed to his request. In a matter of a month he turned on me by accusing me of breaking the rules of our gang. He brought this accusation behind my back to other leaders, who made up the council of the gang.

After their meeting they called me in, and informed me of the accusations and the punishment. I was to be beaten with a large wooden board ten times by each of the five men on the council. This was the first I had heard of these accusations. My "friend" had lied to the council in order to take over the gang before I left the prison. I refused to accept their judgment and punishment. I challenged them and then walked away. I knew the consequences of my actions in this challenge. I could at any time be attacked and perhaps killed.

I returned to my cell, and readied myself for some future attack arming myself as best I could. My cell mate who was a member of the "Latin Kings" saw what I was doing and asked what was wrong. My policy was to keep my business to myself. So I said, "Nothing is wrong." However, he could see that something was very wrong. Being my cell mate he could also be in danger if an attack came into my cell. So he once again asked me stating that he needed to know what was happening. So I told him. He then took the matter to his gang, and they met with the new leader of the "Neta" gang and told them that if anything happened to me they would have to deal with the "Latin Kings."

As I look back on this incident I realize that it was God who protected me. I could have been attacked immediately by the five members of the "Neta" council when I challenged them, and refused their judgment and punishment. God put it in their hearts not to do me any harm. Then the Lord impressed the "Latin Kings" to defend me. How true the scripture is, which says, "Let the heavens be glad, and let the earth rejoice: and let men say among the nations, the LORD reigneth" (1 Chronicles 16:31). God is sovereign ruler in heaven and earth. Even though at the time I was not a Christian, God overruled the plans of the enemy to harm me and perhaps destroy me. God had a purpose for my life, and stopped Satan's plans to hinder God's plan for me.

God actually used my years in prison to preserve my life. You see, back in Puerto Rico a turf war over drug territory broke out soon after I arrived in prison. A former, very dangerous drug dealer who had been in prison for several years returned to my old neighborhood after being released. He wanted his old territory back to sell drugs. By this time my friends were running the drug operations in the area. This man was known to be very dangerous, and would not hesitate to mutilate and kill anyone who got in his way.

So, my friends planned to attack and kill him before he could harm them. If I had been out of prison I would have been right at the forefront of the confrontation with this man, and very well could have been killed myself. My friends set up an ambush and killed him when he was leaving the projects. My state of mind was so twisted that when I heard of the killing I wished I could have been there. It is amazing how evil our thinking can become without the Lord. Satan's plan is always to destroy us or have us destroy others. God's plan is to save us and bring joy into our lives. I now thank the Lord that He intervened in His mysterious way to save my life.

The reason I know my life was saved is that the man my friends killed had friends he had made while in prison who were dealers in other projects. They were loyal to him. So when the news spread that he had been killed they declared war on my friends in my former project. They would come to my project periodically and begin shooting at my friends. A drug war was declared.

In retaliation my friends would go to these shooter's projects and begin shooting at them. This war continued for several years. During that time three of my friends were killed. The first of my friends to be killed was the individual that was my Boston connection who I chose to be loyal to and not incriminate him when I was arrested. He was shot 18 times in the back. That very well could have been me.

Now as I reflect on the many incidences in my life I see God protecting me, and overruling Satan's plans to destroy me. God also has a plan for you. There is a reason you are reading this book. God has brought this book to you for you to learn the lessons I have learned. God has a plan for you also. He wants you to come to know Him as your loving heavenly Father.

I invite you to take a moment and reflect on the times you were saved from harm and even death. Those times were not just coincidences. They were times in which God intervened to save you for the purpose He has for your life. I hope and pray that you will not have to go through the many painful experiences I did before you come to know God. Don't put your life at risk as I did.

The Bible tells us, "... now is the accepted time; behold, now is the day of salvation" (2 Corinthians 6:2). If you are feeling a conviction in your heart to accept Christ, do not delay. Every delay causes us to become a little more hardened, and less receptive to God's call to us. We can come to the point that we do not hear His appeal. You have not reached that point. Why do I say that? I say that because the Lord has led you to read this book.

God continued to intervene to keep me out of trouble even though I did not know Him personally. So when my time came to be released I was able to walk out of the prison a free man. However, the world I was walking into was very different from the one I had spent the past five years in. I was uneducated and unskilled (except in crime). I was angry and had a real "attitude" problem, which got me into trouble many times before. The future didn't look very bright.

CHAPTER FOUR

Life After Prison

When I got out of prison I was very angry. Prison did not rehabilitate me. I figured I did the crime and I did the time. Also, prison life required me to maintain the respect of others. This meant violent behavior when necessary in order to survive. On two occasions I was written up in an "Incident Report" for fighting with another inmate. On one occasion I would have choked one man to death if the guard had not intervened. I was so filled with anger and rage that if someone looked at me the wrong way I was ready to fight them, and would have used anything available to win the confrontation. At that time in my life I had no idea that God could deliver me from the intense feelings of anger that filled me with rage.

My brother had been killed while I was in prison. My pride would have caused me to try to take revenge for his death. I had sworn to my mother that I would kill the guy that took my brother's life. I knew who he was, and even planned how I would do it. He was a fugitive from the law and was in hiding. I was going to kidnap his daughter in order to get him to come to me. When Satan has control of one's mind he leads us into the most diabolical plans. Revenge is never God's way.

My friends in Puerto Rico continued in the drug business. Some of them had been killed, and actually killed each other over jealousies and drug deals gone bad. For these reasons the Lord overruled any desire to return to Puerto Rico. He had other plans for my future.

I had met a woman before I went to prison and fell in love with her. When in prison she was much on my mind and my love for her grew. So when I was released from prison I decided to stay with her. She lived in New Jersey. My mother was in favor of me not returning to Puerto Rico and encouraged me to move to New Jersey. This decision eventually led to me becoming a Christian. God works in our lives in very mysterious ways even when we have no idea that He is leading us. There was no future for me in a relationship with this woman. Yet God used this relationship to lead me to where He wanted me to be. My relationship with her kept me from returning to Puerto Rico.

My mother left everything she had in Puerto Rico in order to move to New Haven, Connecticut, to be close to me. As a result of her move she became a Christian. As I look back, I find it amazing how God can work through such complicated and "bad" situations, and bring it together for the good of His children.

Shortly after I came out of prison the girl I loved suggested that I move to New Haven and stay with my mother. Afterward she would come and join me. She did come for one weekend and then left. I never saw her again. This hurt me very much. However, God was also in this great disappointment. He knew it was not best for her to be in my life. She was just the instrument He used to keep me from going back to Puerto Rico.

I stayed in New Haven and helped my mother pay the bills by working at a regular job. I became restless and wanted to "enjoy" life more. I felt that the past five years in prison had kept me from doing the things I wanted to do. Now I was 23 years old when I got out of prison. So I began going to night clubs, partying, socializing with women, drinking, and using drugs. Every weekend I would get into a fight in the clubs. One thing led to another. Satan works hard to lead us back into his plans for us. I got respect due to my behavior, but the respect was due to the fear others had of me.

Life After Prison

I was working at a steady job and bought a new car. One afternoon after work I got high with a few friends on my block along with getting drunk. I left in my car in this condition. I was listening to "hip hop" music, which inspires anger and violence. The more I listened the more rage and fury I felt. Suddenly my car went out of control and crashed into a wall. I got out and briefly sobered up when I realized what had happened. I called a friend and he came and got me. Smelling alcohol on my breath he gave me gum to chew so when the police came they did not realize I had been drinking.

My car was taken to a repair shop and my friend suggested we go to a downtown club. I was still very high on drugs and very drunk on alcohol. I felt very angry and became enraged when I thought of my car being damaged. I had brought a blade with me to the club. In my rage I pulled it out and began harassing people with it. A youth with some of his friends walked by, and I thought they were going to attack me. So I grabbed him by his head and pulled him toward me and thrust the knife toward his throat. He began begging for his life. At that moment the bouncers grabbed me from the back pulling my arms down causing me to cut the youth's face. The police came, and I was arrested for assault and using a weapon. My life was again headed in the wrong direction.

I was put in the jail in New Haven waiting for bail. When in jail, I once again promised God that I was going to serve Him if He got me out of this problem situation. I meant what I promised. However, I didn't seem to have it in me to keep the promise.

I was released on bail, which was a miracle from God. No one wanted to post bail for me since I was a threat of leaving due to my federal case. One day while in the cell God brought a man to me that asked me why I wasn't out on bail. I told him my situation. He gave me a card of a bail bondsman who might help me. My mother called the name on the card and they agreed to post my bail. So I was released.

During this time I was on probation with the federal government. If I would have been found guilty and imprisoned I would have also had to finish my federal sentence time of four more years. Again the Lord intervened, and I got a year suspended sentence. God had His reasons for keeping me out of prison. We serve a sovereign God who is able to intervene in our behalf as He sees best. God certainly did this many times in my life.

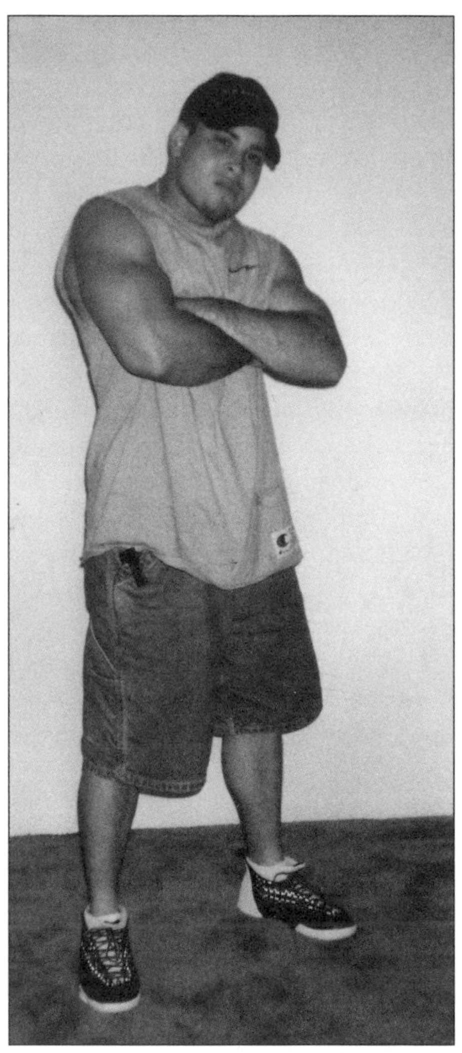
JUAN WITH AN ATTITUDE

God has a plan for our lives, and is more than capable of intervening to protect and direct us. For instance, one day I was traveling the "Q" Bridge on Interstate 95 in New Haven, Connecticut. My friend who was driving the car I was in lost control of the vehicle, which caused us to do a 360-degree spin out on the bridge. The traffic was very heavy, but by God's intervention we did not hit anyone and stopped just before the car was about to go over the bridge into the river. This fall would have killed both of us since the bridge is very high above the water.

On another occasion I was on the block with my boys. I had been drinking and doing drugs. I decided to take a ride through the city in my brand new car. As I was driving down a main street in town I came to a large intersection. Before I realized it I had run through a red light and found myself in the middle of cars going by me on all sides. When I realized this I tried to get out of the way, but a car slammed into the driver side bending my car in the middle by the force of the collision. The impact spun my car around causing it to hit another car. In the process I broke the center console with my hip during the impact, and my two friends received head injuries by hitting the car windows. My injury was minor; only a small bruise on my knee. So I can say from experience, my Lord was watching out for me even before I knew Him.

Before long I was hooked on cocaine, alcohol, marijuana and cigarettes. I took whatever drugs I could get my hands on. I was the kind of person who when I was high on drugs I got mean and was ready to fight. I had all the rage of my brother's murder seething inside me. What had happened to my friends in Puerto Rico also enraged me. It would have been easy for me to return to my old friends in my project. Yet God intervened to keep me in New Haven, Connecticut.

Every time God gave me a break, and I got out of trouble I wanted to straighten out my life. Yet, the rage in me kept moving me back into the wrong life style. I felt deep within myself restlessness. I felt I needed something else in my life, but I didn't know what it was that I needed. Now I realize only God can fill that void. And God in His mysterious way would lead me to that realization in His own way and time.

I kept trying to fill that emptiness in many different ways- drugs, alcohol, and an immoral life-style. I kept high because I didn't want to feel that deep emptiness that was inside me. When I wasn't high I was miserable. I couldn't get along with family, friends or keep a job because of this deep inner pain. I wanted to have a meaningful relationship with a woman, but was unable to. Deep within myself I felt insecure and inadequate. This caused me to experience more anger, and hindered me from developing meaningful relationships. And every failed relationship just added to my rage and feelings of insecurity. Deep depression would come upon me. It is a very painful experience to feel such a deep need within oneself, and not know how to satisfy it. At times I felt like ending my life to escape the pain. That is Satan's plan for all of us. He wants to lead us down his path for us, which will lead to destruction. God's Word describes this condition with the words:

> "There is a way which seemeth right unto a man, but the end thereof are the ways of death. Even in laughter the heart is sorrowful; and the end of that mirth is heaviness." Proverbs 14:12, 13

I thank the Lord that He intervened many times to save me from my own self destruction. What a blessing it is to now know the Lord and experience His love for me. He has filled all the empty places in my life with love, patience, joy, and peace. I now know that only God can do that. Only He can remove the anger, rage, feelings of inadequacy and insecurity. He is able to fill the void in our lives, which will cause the depression and loneliness to leave. I now know that everything I was into before coming to the Lord was Satan's counterfeit solutions, which will ultimately lead to death.

If this is the struggle you are going through right now, God has the answer for you. Simply give your life to God. How can you do that? If you really want to change your life and find true happiness and fulfillment, say the following prayer. "Lord I give my life to you. I ask you to forgive me for all my sins. I accept Jesus Christ as my personal Savior. I ask Jesus to be Lord of my life. Thank You for forgiving me and giving me eternal life. In Jesus' name, amen."

If you said this prayer from your heart truly meaning it, God has heard you and accepted you. Ask Him to fill you with His Holy Spirit, and He will begin filling you with His presence. He will begin filling the empty, painful places in your life with his love. You will have a joy and peace that only God can give. It is important you make this decision for Christ and seek the Spirit's infilling every day.

As you read this you may feel fearful thinking you are not ready to take such a step. You may feel you are too much of a sinner, or that the time is not right. These are all lies of Satan. I can tell you from personal experience. If God forgave me for all my sins and accepted me, I know He will also forgive and accept you.

You may feel you are not ready; it is too big of a step. Remember, when a person joins the military they are not ready to serve in combat at that moment. However, they are trained and prepared for that service. The preparation is a process. Yet, for the process to begin they had to decide to join the military. The same is true for you. You must make the decision to give your life to God. Then He will begin the process in your life. So, being ready is not the issue. What is the issue? Simply making the decision to give your life to God; that is the real issue. That is what God is waiting for.

You are reading this book because God brought it to your attention. Why did He do that? Because He has decided it is time for you to give your life to Him. God has made that decision for you the same way He made it for me. He is calling you right now to accept Jesus and become His child. I know from personal experience that you will never regret making the decision to give the Lord your life and follow Him.

In the past when I was on the street I was "down with" my people. They used to have my back and I had their back (supposedly). Now I understand there are no real friends on the streets. The only true friend you can find is Jesus. So I made a decision, a very important decision. Not to trust another man, but to trust Jesus. That is the reason today I can say I am "down with the King." I am down with Jesus Christ the King of kings and Lord of lords.

Once again I left Connecticut for Puerto Rico. I met my future wife, Alexandra, in a mall. We exchanged phone numbers and called each other. After going on one date I fell head over heels in love with her. There was no other woman for me.

Have you ever experienced that? Are you going through something like that right now? I know how you feel. I have been there and done that. So, listen up!

After the first date I returned to Connecticut. However, because I was so hooked up on Alexandra all I did was think about her. So I decided to save some money and go back to Puerto Rico to be closer to her. Little did I know that when I arrived there she would reject me. So when I met her in Puerto Rico we went to a hotel lobby and she broke it down to me. She said she just wanted to be friends and that was it. I stood there in amazement saying to her, "What did you say?" Can you imagine that happening after I came all the way to Puerto Rico to meet her? I left my job and my home planning to make a life with her, and she "dumped" me just like that. That hurts!

After Alexandra told me that she wasn't interested in a close, permanent relationship I got frustrated and mad. I decided to go to a bar and drink my sorrows away. There were some guys in the bar playing dominos. I started provoking them. They ignored me for a while, but I was persistent. Finally all of a sudden they jumped on me and we got into a fight. The six of them and I were going at it when one of them hit me from behind with a chair, which dropped me to the floor.

I got up quickly and challenged them to come on at me. I then saw five of them split and one stayed. When I looked at him I saw him pulling his shirt up and pull out a gun. He was no more than four feet from me. I quickly turned away running. Immediately I heard the shots behind me. The bullets were flying by my head and all around me. I didn't realize it, but one hit me. I kept running to my sister-in-law's house. I loudly knocked on the door and she let me in. When inside I began feeling light-headed, I began checking to see if I had been hit and felt wet on my left hip.

The bullet went through my hip exiting my buttocks. Therefore, there were two bullet holes that were bleeding.

Alexandra found out I had been shot. God used her to give me advice. She suggested I move to Florida and stay with my father. So, I took her advice and moved in with my father. At that time my father was attending the Seventh-day Adventist church. He began talking to me about Jesus and took me to church with him. As the months passed by I began making new friends in the area and started going out to the clubs, which was not a good decision. I began hanging out with the wrong kind of people again. In a matter of a couple months I was back into drugs and getting into fights. That took me away from church activities.

Soon I began getting into trouble again. One day on the way to work the driver and I were smoking marijuana. A cop stopped us and smelling the drugs asked us to get out of the car. I always carried a knife and when the officer patted me down he found the knife, which was illegal due to its length. It was considered a concealed weapon. They let my driver friend go. However, because of the knife they took me to jail. Here I was locked up again after being in Florida less than a year.

My father bailed me out, and I was put on state probation. I had just gotten off federal probation, and now I found myself back on probation again. Even in this God was working to bring me where He wanted me to be. He certainly works in mysterious ways even when we don't know He is working in our behalf.

The probation officer appointed to my case was a Christian lady. She became a real friend to me. Her intentions were to help me by sharing Christ with me. She even told me that she felt the Spirit of God when she met me, and said God had plans for me. I met with her every other month. So we had a chance to develop a relationship. She invited me to church, and to her house to meet her family. She even told me I was going to be an evangelist someday. God began talking to me about His future plans for me through this lady.

At that time I was living with a girl friend, which was a very non-Christian home. Instead of Christ there were drugs, fights, ghetto music, alcohol, etc. So as usual I was involved again with the wrong kind of activities.

One day I was hanging with my friends in a project. I was smoking marijuana and drinking alcohol. In that condition on my way home to the apartment a police officer drove up behind me and pulled me over. He said I was weaving from one lane to another. He asked me for my license and registration. When I gave them to him he smelled the alcohol and asked me if I had been drinking. I said, "Yes, I have been drinking, but only had a couple beers." He asked me to get out of the car. I obeyed. He said he was going to test me for alcohol. He said I didn't pass the test, and said he was going to arrest me. He began handcuffing me. I began thinking that I would go back to jail because I was on probation. So, I looked at him and said that he had not given me the sobriety test. He then became violent and threw me against the car.

Being in handcuffs, I put my leg between me and the car to keep my face from being jammed into the car. At that he picked me up and body slammed me against the sidewalk causing a large gash in my head. Other officers came and joined in by putting their feet on me pressing me to the ground even though I was not resisting arrest. One put his foot on my neck so hard that I could not breathe. I thought I was going to die and my life passed before me. I became so fearful that I began pleading for my life. All my life, even during the bad times, I felt God was protecting me. However, at that moment I felt He had left me, and I was totally without protection.

They took me to the hospital, and I received 12 staples for my head gash. They then took me to the jail. This time my mother bailed me out, and I went back to my girlfriend's house. Something happened to me that night that changed my life forever. A severe battle began taking place between God and Satan in my life. Satan wanted to kill me by causing me to get so discouraged that

I wanted to kill myself. This battle went on for five months. At the end of the five months I made my decision to give my life to the Lord.

Again Jesus' hand reached out and pulled me out of the situation. How many times has Jesus pulled you out, and then you found yourself back in the same bad situation? How many times has Jesus or a loved one forgiven you and you again and again let them down? If you are going through that same kind of situation and you are trying to get your life together, but keep falling back don't give up on yourself. Remember, Jesus never gives up on you. His hand will always be reaching out to you to bring you out of the mess you find yourself in again and again.

I tell you this because that is exactly what I went through. Satan wants you to think that you are no good and will never accomplish anything. He wants to discourage you, make you feel low, unloved, and lead you to despair to the point of even wanting to kill yourself. Jesus said,

> "The thief cometh not, but for to steal, and to kill, and to destroy: I am come that they might have life, and that they might have it more abundantly." John 10:10

Satan is the thief and his plan is always to lead you to destruction. Jesus' plan is for you to have the abundant life. That's the honest truth. Satan did his best to destroy me, but Jesus intervened to save me. I thank Him for not giving up on me. God tells you,

> " 'For I know the plans I have for you,' declares the LORD, 'plans to prosper you and not to harm you, plans to give you hope and a future.' " Jeremiah 29:11, NIV

Jesus used my probation officer to keep pulling me out of bad situations. I began going to church with this lady, and asking God to help me change my life. One day when I went to church with her, and afterward came back to the house where I was staying my girlfriend gave me a 40 ounce beer. I grabbed it, opened it, but before I took a sip of it I began thinking about God.

I was strongly convicted not to drink it. So I went outside and threw the bottle of beer on the street and told her I was never going to drink again. That day I went back into a small room in the house, and fell on the floor and began crying out to the Lord. I was praying and crying pouring out my heart. I was telling Him the way I felt and that I wanted to surrender my life to Him. I said, "God if you want me to serve You, You need to take me out of this house right away."

The next day my prayer was answered. I woke up early and asked my girlfriend to take me to my father's house. I had let my father down so many times that he had given up on me. However, when she dropped me off at his house and I asked him to help me, God changed his heart toward me. He made a phone call and made arrangements for me to get a room in a rooming house. He made a second phone call and found me a job in a mechanic's shop even though I didn't know anything about mechanics. God was clearly touching people's hearts for me in order to pull me out of the mess I had put myself in.

This was finally the turning point in my life. From that time forward my life was turned around for Jesus. The Bible says,

> "He that covereth his sins shall not prosper: but whoso confesseth and forsaketh them shall have mercy." Proverbs 28:13

I have found this verse to be true. As soon as I was honest with God and confessed and by His grace forsook my sins He began prospering me. My life began being changed for the better. God wants to prosper you also. However, for this to happen you must make the decision to be honest with Him; confess the sins you have committed and turn from them by giving your life to Him. Your life will never be the same again. If you are tired, worried and your life doesn't make any sense or doesn't seem to be going anywhere I have some advice for you. Jesus said,

> "Come unto me, all ye that labour and are heavy laden, and I will give you rest." Matthew 11:28

CHAPTER FIVE

My Brother's Killer

I was born in the United States, and lived on the East coast for ten years before moving to Puerto Rico. I had three brothers. My older brother, Ivan, and I were raised together. Being older, he was my role model. Even more than that, he was like a father to me since my father and mother had separated when I was around four years old. Ivan and I were very close. We went to church together, and hung out together in the neighborhood.

My brother became a member of a gang when he was 15 years old. That caused him to drift away from the Lord and church. He soon got involved with drinking, partying and bad influences. Sometimes when he came to our house to visit I could smell the alcohol. My mother also found drugs he had been using. On some occasions I would see blood on his pants and shirts, that wasn't his. So I was exposed at an early age to the gangs, and began accepting that way of life especially since I looked up to my brother. In the 1970s and '80s there was a resurgence of gangs in the states.

When I was growing up my mother's husband was an alcoholic. He would get drunk and argue with my mother. He was also into drugs, and was a troublemaker. He didn't want to work, and depended on my mother to take care of him. At times he would come home and physically abuse her. My brother would come to her defense.

On one occasion when he attacked my mother my older brother came into the room. He then started arguing with my brother, and broke an electric guitar over his forearm when my brother was protecting himself from being hit in the head. My other two younger brothers came into the room. My three brothers then attacked my stepfather, and my mother hit him over the head with a glass coffee pot. I was the youngest of the four of us, about seven years old, and became so afraid that I ran to the bathroom and vomited. These kind of events happened on numerous occasions. So, I was exposed to violence in our home at an early age.

As time passed the fights continued in my home, and my brother continued in the gangs. My mother was concerned about his safety so she sent him to Puerto Rico to live with his birth father. When he got there he and his father constantly fought. Therefore, he moved in with a girl friend, and had three children with her.

My stepfather cheated on my mother with another woman. My mother didn't realize the affair was happening until one day he told her he was moving out of the house to live with this woman, and move with her to Puerto Rico. My mother and I followed him to Puerto Rico and lived in the projects. She was hoping to get him back. He did eventually return to my mother. However, the fighting continued. So I continued to live in a very violent environment both in the home and outside the home in the projects.

My mother knew the projects were violent and urged me not to fight, fearful that I might fight a kid whose father was a violent drug dealer and as a family we could face serious consequences. However, since I was new in the projects I literally had to fight in order to keep from being beat up every day by guys in the project. It was a matter of keeping my position among these guys. That was the only way to gain respect and be accepted.

I was ten years old when we moved to the projects. From then on I was constantly confronted with violence. As the years went on I became more and more violent and even initiated confrontations.

Satan wanted violent behavior to control me. His ultimate goal was to kill me. I thank God that He was watching over me even when I knew little of Him or understood His will for me. I know that my violent past has left its mark on me. Even though I am a Christian at times Satan tries to cause me to become angry and violent. I realize what a blessing it is to not grow up in this kind of environment. Sin leaves its scars. The apostle Paul described the battle the scars of sin leaves with the words,

> "I do not understand what I do. For what I want to do I do not do, but what I hate I do. And if I do what I do not want to do, I agree that the law is good. As it is, it is no longer I myself who do it, but it is sin living in me. I know that nothing good lives in me, that is, in my sinful nature.
>
> "For I have the desire to do what is good, but I cannot carry it out. For what I do is not the good I want to do; no, the evil I do not want to do—this I keep on doing. Now if I do what I do not want to do, It is no longer I who do it, but it is sin living in me that does it.
>
> "So I find this law at work: When I want to do good, evil is right there with me. For in my inner being I delight in God's law; but I see another law at work in the members of my body, waging war against the law of my mind and making me a prisoner of the law of sin at work within my members. What a wretched man I am! Who will rescue me from this body of death? Thanks be to God—through Jesus Christ our Lord! ..." Romans 7:15-25, NIV

These verses describe the struggle the Christian has. We all have a sinful nature. In my case, the violent part of that nature was developed and became strong during my childhood. I never killed anyone, but was very capable of doing that terrible sin, and came close to doing it several times. I thank God that He kept me from that extreme act of violence.

I can identify with Paul's words quoted above. Even today when someone looks at me wrong or shows me disrespect I feel the violence trying to emerge within me and control me. It is only by a personal relationship with God through prayer, serious study of God's Word and constant communion with Him that we can experience His grace and not be controlled by our sinful nature. Paul goes on to tell us,

> "... count yourselves dead to sin but alive to God in Christ Jesus. Therefore do not let sin reign in your mortal body so that you obey its evil desires. Do not offer the parts of your body to sin, as instruments of wickedness, but rather offer yourselves to God, as those who have been brought from death to life; and offer the parts of your body to him as instruments of righteousness. For sin shall not be your master, because you are not under law, but under grace." Romans 6:11-14, NIV

Therefore, the only way we can be free from our sinful nature is to give ourselves to God everyday to serve Him, and to learn how to serve others in love. We must die to our old sinful self every day. Again Paul describes this experience.

> "I have been crucified with Christ and I no longer live, but Christ lives in me. The life I live in the body, I live by faith in the Son of God, who loved me and gave himself for me." Galatians 2:20

It is not in our own strength we can live the Christian life. No. It is only in Christ's strength that we can obey God. When we are tempted we must turn immediately to Christ, and ask Him to give us the victory and believe He will. Paul writes:

My Brother's Killer

"I can do everything through him [Christ] who gives me strength." Philippians 4:13, NIV

As for my life, by God's grace, I will use the energy and life I once used for serving the sinful nature to serve Christ with every ounce of life that is within me. When I lived in the projects, and was involved in the gangs I was willing to give my all, even to the point of death, for the gang values. Now, I thank God, for giving me a "new heart and mind." He has given me the opportunity to serve Him and if necessary to the point of death also.

"For to me, to live is Christ and to die is gain." Philippians 1:21, NIV

My older brother was a skilled bass player and was a member of a musical group. He invited me to go along with the group as a "bag boy" to help with equipment. When one of the singers wasn't able to perform the group asked me to sing since my brother had heard me sing around the house. He realized I seemed to have the ability. I agreed to sing with the group. However, since I didn't know the choreography, they had me sing in the back of the band. In time I became the lead singer.

My brother, Ivan, in his prime

As I reflect on this experience how wonderful it

would have been if we had been singing and playing music for the Lord. Our music could have been a great blessing to others and give God praises. That is God's will for all who sing or play music. The psalmist tells us to, "Praise the LORD with the harp; make music to him on the ten-stringed lyre. Sing to him a new song; play skillfully, and shout for joy" (Psalm 33:2, 3, NIV).

Now I know that the Lord deserves all our praise. He is so loving and merciful toward His children. He watches over us and protects us. It is important that we praise with our words, songs and music. The angels of heaven praise Him often for His goodness. John the Revelator wrote of what he saw with the words; "Then I heard every creature in heaven and on earth and under the earth and on the sea, and all that is in them, singing: 'To him who sits on the throne and to the lamb be praise and honor and glory and power, for ever and ever!" (Revelation 5:13, NIV).

What a contrast is the popular music of today. Satan uses music very skillfully to lead young and old away from God. The words of popular "hip hop, reggaeton, pop rock and Latin music" all lead away from God and into the evils of this world. When we listen to or participate in this music it strongly affects us to become violent, immoral, and leads deeper into Satan's game, which will always lead to death if followed to its natural end.

It was my participation in this music that led me to begin using alcohol, cocaine, and other drugs. In order to really be a part of the music group I sang with I began using drugs to stay "high" with them. Otherwise I would not have been as connected with the other members, and feel a part of the group.

The Bible tells us Satan was the music director in heaven. So he knows very well the power of music for good or bad. God wants music to be a blessing to us. Satan wants music to lead us away from God, and into the most vile and destructive experiences of life.

So, if you are serious about finding real joy and peace in your life through giving your life to God, it is essential that you turn away from the music of Satan. You cannot serve God and Satan at the same time.

My brother was nine years older than me. So he would look out for me. Anytime I was in trouble in school he would show me how to defend myself.

Ivan wasn't a drug dealer. However, he was very street wise. He taught me how to survive on the streets. He learned karate and was good at it. So I learned from him how to fight and hold my own against almost anyone who tried to intimidate me.

In time I felt the band was not treating me fairly. They kept paying me as a "bag boy" instead of paying me as one of the lead singers of the band. Therefore, I began moving away from the band and spending more time with "my boys" in the project.

When I left the music business and returned to my friends in the project they had already begun selling drugs. I saw how easy it was for them to make money. So I very soon got involved in the drug business.

As an example of the violent experiences Satan was leading me into, I will share the following story. A friend of mine had been beaten up over a basketball game that took place out of our project. You know what that means? They showed us disrespect, which meant we had to take care of business. He came to me and my friends and told us what had happened. So we gathered together about 15 of us and went to the area where this had happened. We had bats and even guns with us. However, we didn't plan to use the guns. When we arrived we saw four guys, one sitting on a car and three on a bench. We asked where the guy was that beat up our friend. The guy on the car said he wasn't there, and that we had to come back tomorrow. This was a put-down, which enraged us.

One of our guys hit the guy who said that with a golf club on the front of his forehead knocking him out instantly. Several of our guys began beating him. The other three began running. One of them ran right into me. I grabbed him and began hitting him in the face and anywhere else I could. Others joined me in the beating. In that moment he managed to get away from us briefly. My brother quickly hit him in the head with a bat that threw him against a steel fence that was about ten feet from us. He began holding his head, moaning and begging for mercy. We were all filled with rage and out of control. My brother ran to the guy and began hitting him again with the bat in the ribs. We could hear his ribs cracking. He became unconscious. We hung him by his jacket on the steel fence and left him bleeding.

I hesitate to relate this experience. However, it clearly makes the point of the terrible consequences of becoming involved in drugs, gangs, and satanic music, etc. Satan takes over those who do such things and there is no limit to the violent and immoral things they will do. I am ashamed that I ever participated in such activities. I wish I could go back and stop the experience from happening. I know I can't do that. I know God has forgiven me for the many wrong things I have done. I thank God for the promise, "If we confess our sins, he is faithful and just to forgive our sins and cleanse us from all unrighteousness" (1 John 1:9).

My appeal to you is to think seriously about the direction your life is going. You are reading this book for a reason. God has led you to it. There is no sin you have committed that is too terrible that God cannot forgive. It is not too late for you to give your life to God and turn your life around.

We will face everything we have done in the judgment before God someday. The Bible tells us, "Be happy, young man, while you are young, and let your heart give you joy in the days of your youth. Follow the ways of your heart and whatever your eyes see, but know that for all these things God will bring you to judgment" (Ecclesiastes 11:9, NIV).

What does that mean? What goes around comes around. I have experienced that in very painful ways. I have shed many tears and have had much suffering. What have I suffered? Let me tell you.

The greatest loss in my life was the death of my brother. I found out about his death while I was in prison. One day I called my mother. A friend of my mother answered the phone and said my mother wasn't there. Then I asked to speak with my brother. They started passing the phone to different people to speak with me. Then I knew something was wrong. One of my mother's friends told me that my brother had been shot and killed the night before in front of our home in Puerto Rico.

I later learned when my brother was shot he and his girl friend were walking to my mother's door. The killer was my brother's girl friend's ex-husband. Previously this man and my brother had gotten into a fight, and he had been badly beaten by my brother. So he decided to lay in wait by hiding in the stairway of the apartment complex. When my brother approached, the killer came up behind him and said, "Isn't that nice," and then shot him in the back giving my brother no chance to defend himself or run. It was a very cowardly act.

Two of the bullets hit my brother in the back killing him instantly. Two other bullets went through the front door almost killing my mother. God chose to let my brother die that day. However, He chose to let my mother live. God has His reasons for allowing things to happen as they do. It is important we remember that lesson throughout life. Many things will happen to

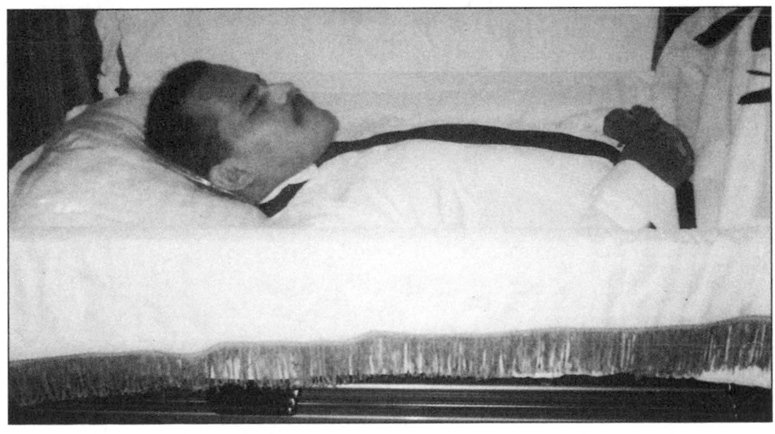

My brother Ivan's funeral

us that we don't understand. We must learn to trust God, knowing that He is a loving Father and working all things out for our good (Romans 8:28).

When my mother opened the door she saw her dead son on his back looking her straight into her eyes. She was so horrified that her loud screams could be heard blocks away.

When I received the news I lost it; I mentally blacked out and began screaming and hitting the walls. I had a confrontation with one of the correction officers, who tried to settle me down. I was in the prison unit and when he approached me, in my rage I shoved him. After that the unit was put into lockdown for fear of more violence.

They planned to put me into segregation. However, some of the other inmates told the officers that I had just learned that my brother had been killed. The officers then decided to put me in the hospital instead. When in the hospital and months later while still in prison I would continue to break down in tears over his death. I couldn't believe he was dead. I asked my attorney if I could be escorted to the funeral. He said no, which hurt me deeply and made me even more enraged. At that moment I made a promise to myself that I was going to kill the guy who killed my brother. I knew him well and began planning my strategy. I had many friends in Puerto Rico, and could easily have gotten a gun and set up a situation to kill him. I know nothing would have been said if I killed him. The law of the street is "hear nothing, see nothing and say nothing." I could have gotten away with his murder.

I thank the Lord that He once again intervened and kept me from doing that terrible act of revenge. The Bible clearly tells us never to take vengeance on another no matter what they have done to us or our family.

> "Dearly beloved, avenge not yourselves, but rather give place unto wrath: for it is written, Vengeance is mine; I will repay, saith the Lord. Therefore if thine enemy hunger,

> feed him; if he thirst, give him drink … Be not overcome of evil, but overcome evil with good." Romans 12:19-21

Jesus also instructed us concerning dealing with our enemies.

> "Ye have heard that it hath been said, Thou shalt love thy neighbour, and hate thine enemy. But I say unto you, Love your enemies, bless them that curse you, do good to them that hate you, and pray for them which despitefully use you, and persecute you." Matthew 5:43, 44

Vengeance and hatred are terrible things to have in our heart. They will destroy the vessel they are in. When we hate someone and want to take vengeance for what they have done to us it is like taking poison and waiting for the other person to die. It is foolish and will lead only to heartache and further pain. Bitterness is very destructive to the one who harbors it. The Bible is very clear. Those who choose to continue to harbor bitterness in their heart will be eternally lost.

> "Follow peace with all men, and holiness, without which no man shall see the Lord: Looking diligently lest any man fail of the grace of God; lest any root of bitterness springing up trouble you, and thereby many be defiled." Hebrews 12:14, 15

It is not just the non-Christian who has a struggle with bitterness. There are many counsels in the Bible instructing us to avoid all forms of bitterness and hatred toward anyone. Instead we are to forgive everyone no matter what they have done. If we do not forgive, we will not be forgiven by God for our sins.

> "And when ye stand praying, forgive, if ye have ought against any: that your Father also which is in heaven

may forgive you your trespasses. But if ye do not forgive, neither will your Father which is in heaven forgive your trespasses." Mark 11:25, 26

Before I became a Christian I could have never forgiven the murderer of my brother. My anger caused many sorrows in my life, my head was split open in a fight, was shot, almost killed many times and imprisoned. My mother had lost her son through violence. So she also suffered much due to my brother's anger and violent behavior. Anger and violence not only hurts the person themselves, but also brings suffering to loved ones and friends.

I have been amazed at what the grace of God can do in one's life. After I became a Christian God removed all anger and bitterness toward the man who killed my brother. When I think of him now, I have no harsh feelings toward him. In fact, God has led me to pray for him hoping that someday he too will find the loving, merciful heavenly Father I have found. I pray that he will accept Jesus and have the hope of eternal life. My mother feels as I do about the man who so violently took her son away from her.

Recently we received a letter telling us that this man, who is now imprisoned for killing my brother, is trying to appeal his sentence to reduce it. The authorities gave us the opportunity to appeal to the courts not to release him. However, because of the forgiveness God has put in our hearts we decided not to write an appeal to counter his request. We hold no hard feelings toward him. We are leaving his future with God.

I know you too have had suffering in your life. You may feel deep anger and bitterness toward someone. I appeal to you, give your life to the Lord. By His grace you too can forgive whatever has been done to hurt you.

CHAPTER SIX

How I Changed

My change from being an angry, violent, drug dealing individual to becoming a new person who had accepted Christ was a process. As I look back I can see God leading me to the point of genuine transformation from a violent man to a servant of the King of kings.

Since I was a child I knew of Jesus because I had been taken to church by my mother for many years. Many children and youth who go to church simply go because their parents want them to attend or go for social reasons, or as a routine, but do not know Christ as their personal Savior.

To become a Christian one must have a personal encounter with God that becomes a life changing event. This will change everything from one's language, music, dress, friends and much more. They will desire to pray, study God's Word, and speak the Word to others. This will become their great desire and passion. If you find yourself attending church, but have not had a life changing encounter with God I invite you to ask God to come into your life and reveal Himself to you. He will always hear that prayer, and reveal Himself to you. You life will never be the same when that happens.

When I came out of prison I thought my life would be changed, and I would have freedom and happiness. I was mistaken. Jesus said,

Transformed by the Spirit

> "Peace I leave with you, my peace I give unto you: not as the world giveth, give I unto you. Let not your heart be troubled, neither let it be afraid." John 14:27

I thought "I" could achieve the happiness I wanted. However, I discovered that was impossible. God did not create us to find peace apart from Him. We were created to be in close relationship with God Himself. It is only in a close relationship with God that we find joy and peace. So, the more I tried to find peace in the world the more I found myself going deeper and deeper into depression, frustration and loneliness. My inner pain was so great that often after returning home from going to a club seeking a good time I would feel empty the next day. I felt very lonely and insecure. I would go into the bathroom and begin crying in the bathtub. I wanted peace, but didn't know how to get it. How true the scripture is which states:

> "There is a way which seemeth right unto a man, but the end thereof are the ways of death. Even in laughter the heart is sorrowful; and the end of that mirth is heaviness." Proverbs 14:12, 13

My laughter at the parties always turned to sorrow and heaviness the next day. I went to the parties and clubs seeking inner peace and joy not realizing that can never be found there. Instead, all I found was fighting, drunkenness and trouble.

Jesus said,

> "Come unto me, all ye that labour and are heavy laden, and I will give you rest." Matthew 11:28

Today I have found those words of Jesus to be true. When I accepted Christ I found the peace I was looking for. The empty space I was trying to fill by the things of the world is now filled with the presence of Jesus. My insecurity has been replaced with great security in Christ as my Lord. I finally found the purpose God has had for my life all along. He has a purpose for each of us. It is only as we have a personal encounter with God and accept Christ as our Savior that God's purpose will be satisfaction in our life. Only then will we find true meaning and fulfillment in life. As long as we keep trying on our own to find peace in the world we will never find it. However, when we stop trying then God can start working within us to fill the emptiness with His presence. So, if you feel like I did empty, lonely, insecure and trying to get approval, I invite you to give your life to God. When you know you have His approval nothing else matters.

How do you get His approval? When you accept Christ as your Savior you are approved by God.

> "Therefore being justified by faith, we have peace with God through our Lord Jesus Christ." Romans 5:1

The disciples James and John were called sons of thunder by Jesus because of their quick temper. Then as they came to know Jesus and accept Him their lives were completely changed. John became known as the disciple of love. James became a great, diplomatic leader of the church.

Peter was quick tempered and eager to avenge himself or Jesus when attacked. When the crowd came to take Jesus in the garden Peter attacked the high priest's servant with a knife trying to cut his head off, but cut his ear off instead. Peter became so changed by being filled with the presence of Jesus through receiving the baptism of the Holy Spirit on the Day of Pentecost that he became a great shepherd of God's people. God's presence was so strong in Peter that when his shadow passed over sick people they were healed.

The God Who changed Peter, James and John can change you also. It doesn't matter how angry, bitter, and insecure you are God can give you great peace and fulfill the glorious plan he has for your life. No matter how bad your past has been God is willing to forgive you. The great apostle Paul had been instrumental in killing Christians. When he gave his life to Jesus he became a powerful servant of God, and God worked many miracles through him.

The saying is true, "God is a bigger forgiver than the biggest sinner." No sin is too big for God to forgive. I personally know that truth about God. I have shared some of my past with you. If God can forgive me He can forgive anyone, even you.

My life was going from bad to worse. I had been in and out of prison. I continued to get in trouble with the police. As previously mentioned, at one time I was thrown to the ground by the police, which caused my head to be split open. At that moment my life flashed before my eyes. I realized I could die right then and there. Even during all my terrible activities I felt God was protecting me. Now all of a sudden I felt alone and totally unprotected by God or anyone. I became very frightened and even paranoid. I cried out to the police, "Don't kill me!"

I went to jail for a week after this encounter with the police. While in jail I thought a lot about the experience. I met a man who was sentenced to life. Something clicked in my mind; I had to change my life completely. However, I knew I could not do it on my own. I had tried that before and it didn't work.

So after I got out of jail I went to my room and fell on my knees in prayer. I said; "God, I surrender my life to You. If I don't give it to you I'm going to lose it." At that moment I asked God to take me out of the place I was living because of the environment. I knew I could not serve the Lord there.

The next day I awoke early, which was unusual for me. I told the girl where I was living to give me a ride to my father's house. I had let him down many times and he had given up on me. As I approached his house I didn't know how he would receive me. I knocked on the door. He opened the door and invited me in. I asked him to help me. He just looked at me not saying anything. God touched his heart and he made a phone call and found me a room to live in. He made a second phone call and found me a job. So the Lord was already working in my life in answer to my prayer. This began my new life in Christ.

I was serious about my commitment to the Lord. After that prayer I had given up the immoral life style, drugs, alcohol, and smoking within two months. I wanted nothing to do with my old life. It was a battle to get rid of the smoking. However, I found that I could have the victory through Christ. Paul in the Bible tells us,

> "I can do all things through Christ which strengtheneth me." Philippians 4:13

When I made my commitment to the Lord Satan didn't give up on me. I found myself confronted on several occasions with women Satan brought to me who actually propositioned me to have sex with them. For example, the job I got was working in a garage. One day a woman came in wanting an oil change, but did not have any money. So she suggested that she could come by my apartment later to give herself to me for payment. She was very attractive and the temptation was very appealing. Satan knows exactly how to tempt us. A few days later two other women from my past came suggesting we have a threesome. This kind of thing happened again and again. Yet, by God's grace I was determined to be faithful to Him.

The Bible story of David and Bathsheba clearly points out the danger of a man allowing his desires to overrule what he knows God's will is for him. In David's case his yielding to his sexual desires led to adultery and murder. Samson is another case where a man of God allowed his lustful desires for a woman he should have never been involved with to lead him away from God, and limited the ministry the Lord wanted to accomplish through him.

The house I moved into was a large 30 room home that housed migrant workers. When I moved there it was not the season for migrant workers. Therefore I was all alone in the house. I was somewhat afraid being alone in such a large house, which was also isolated in the woods. So I would sleep with a light on.

I began praying to the Lord to get me out of this large, empty house. It was a very lonely place. The Lord works in mysterious ways. He moved me out of the house within one week. The Lord used a $700.00 refund my attorney gave me when she decided not to continue representing me, in my case against the police department that caused my head injury.

I went to work the same day I received the $700.00 refund, and a lady came to the garage where I worked stating that she had some apartments for rent. I asked her if I could see one of them. So she showed me the apartment, and I was able to use the $700.00 as a deposit in order to rent the apartment. I was amazed how the Lord once again worked to answer my prayer. He not only gave me another apartment, but a much better place than I was staying. Now I wasn't isolated and lonely.

Sometimes Satan uses isolation and loneliness to make it more difficult to follow the Lord. I have learned it is important for every Christian, especially new Christians, to develop new friendships with fellow Christians. If this does not happen it will be easy for the new Christian to reconnect with their old friends, and find themselves back in the old lifestyle of immorality, alcohol and drugs. This can happen, for this is exactly what happened to me when I previously tried to give my life to the Lord. However, it is important the new Christian be patient. It may take time for new friendships to be made with other Christians. Yet, I know if we ask God to lead us into the right relationships with Christians who will be a blessing to us He will answer that prayer in His own way and time.

The rent in this my apartment was more than my room in the large house. My job at the garage paid me much less than the monthly rent for the apartment. My boss said he could not pay me any more money. Yet, I believed the Lord had provided the apartment. So, I had faith he would provide the extra money needed. My boss was somewhat hardhearted when it came to money. God worked a miracle once again for me. He moved upon the heart of my boss and led him to pay me enough money for the next three months so I would have enough to pay for my rent.

I had been learning the lesson that Jesus taught when He told us not to worry about the necessities of life. He taught that we should put God first and then everything we need will be provided.

> "Therefore I say unto you, Take no thought for your life, what ye shall eat, or what ye shall drink; nor yet for your body, what ye shall put on. Is not the life more than meat, and the body than raiment? Behold the fowls of the air: for they sow not, neither do they reap, nor gather into barns; yet your heavenly Father feedeth them. Are ye not much better than they? Which of you by taking thought can add one cubit unto his stature? And why take ye thought for raiment? Consider the lilies of the field, how they grow; they toil not, neither do they spin: And yet I say unto you, that even Solomon in all his glory was not arrayed like one of these.
>
> "Wherefore, if God so clothe the grass of the field, which to day is, and to morrow is cast into the oven, shall he not much more clothe you, O ye of little faith? Therefore take no thought, saying, What shall we eat? or, What shall we drink? or, Wherewithal shall we be clothed? (For after all these things do the Gentiles seek:) for your heavenly Father knoweth that ye have need of all these things. But seek ye first the kingdom of God, and his righteousness; and all these things shall be added unto you." Matthew 6:25-33

I chose to trust the Lord believing He would provide for me. His Word proved to be true. God provided the apartment and the money for the security deposit and rent for three months. I didn't have any of this money, and did not know how I would get it. I had surrendered to God and trusted Him to provide what I needed to follow Him. Getting out of the large, empty house was necessary for me. Therefore, I trusted God to open way for me to move. The Lord has promised not to let those who give their lives to Him become destitute.

The Lord actually gives His followers three promises-eternal life, health and prosperity. We find one such promise in the disciple John's third letter.

> "Beloved, I wish above all things that thou mayest prosper and be in health, even as thy soul prospereth." 3 John 2

If we don't achieve these it is because we are not following our Lord in some area of our life. For example, in the area of health, if I become a Christian and choose to keep taking drugs and alcohol I will be doing things that actually are destroying my health. The Lord will lead His followers to understand principles of health so they can cooperate with Him in achieving good health. In my case the Lord led me to stop all drugs, alcohol, tobacco and even become a vegetarian following a meatless diet.

It is a serious thing to disregard God's counsels in any area of our life. He wants us to do our best to obey His instructions so we can glorify Him by the way we live.

> "Whether therefore ye eat, or drink, or whatsoever ye do, do all to the glory of God." 1 Corinthians 10:31

This instruction from God applies to every area of our life-how we dress, the food we eat, what we drink, the music we listen to, the shows we watch, who we hang out with, what we read, what we let our mind dwell on—everything we do should properly represent God in our life.

I had no money for furniture. I would sleep on the floor in the bedroom. But as I said before; we serve a loving Father who will provide for all our needs. If we are faithful to Him He will be faithful to us. I proved this to myself when it came to finances. When I became a Christian I decided to follow God's instruction and begin giving Him tithes and offerings from the small income I was making. I chose to believe God's promise that says.

> "Bring ye all the tithes into the storehouse, that there may be meat in mine house, and prove me now herewith, saith the LORD of hosts, if I will not open you the windows of heaven, and pour you out a blessing, that there shall not be room enough to receive it. And I will rebuke the devourer for your sakes, and he shall not destroy the fruits of your ground; neither shall your vine cast her fruit before the time in the field, saith the LORD of hosts. And all nations shall call you blessed: for ye shall be a delightsome land, saith the LORD of hosts." Malachi 3:10-12

Even though I did not earn a lot of money I decided to give God ten percent of it for tithe and also gave an offering above the tithe. I have learned that we cannot out give the Lord. As we are faithful to Him He will be faithful to us in every way, even in the area of money, love, material things, and spiritual blessings.

Within a couple months after being in my new apartment God provided all the furniture I needed such as a bed, living room set, TV, VCR, DVD player, microwave, and even a car. People would come up to me and offer money and food. I can tell you from experience; God wants to prosper you and bless you. Some Christians think poverty is holiness. God does not want his children to be in poverty. He wants to bless us with even more than we need so we can in turn be a blessing to others with the money, and other material things God has blessed us with. Our goal in life should not to become rich. Rather our goal should be to be faithful to God, and leave it with Him as to how much He chooses to bless us with. Then use what we have to bless others.

God wants to open the way for His children to be placed in high places in society, government, and business, etc. So, I challenge you to give your life to God, follow Him as He leads you and don't be afraid of going where God leads even if it seems impossible. For example, I never thought I would be speaking to hundreds of people in different countries about the Lord. As God opened the way for me it was important I trust Him and follow where He leads. Wherever He leads or whatever He asks us to do He will prepare us so we will be able to do what He asks.

It is important the Christian realize that he has an important role to play when it comes to success in life and in God's work. It is important we not give up when times get tough in life or in our walk with the Lord. In the Old Testament there is the story of Joseph the son of Jacob. His brothers hated him and sold him as a slave to a caravan going to Egypt. In Egypt he was sold to a good man and God blessed all Joseph did. Then his master's wife falsely accused Joseph of sexual assault. As a result Joseph was thrown into prison.

Then through the release of one of the prisoners, who knew God led Joseph to interpret dreams, Joseph was asked to interpret a dream that Pharaoh had. Joseph interpreted the dream and was put in authority right next to Pharaoh. Joseph became the second most powerful man in Egypt, which was one of the most powerful nations in the world at that time. Joseph did not let himself become discouraged by difficult circumstances. He chose to trust God, and God used these difficult situations to lead him to the high position He wanted him in. If there had not been a slave sale, and if there had not be an imprisonment there would not have been a governorship for Joseph right next to the king.

This is an important lesson for each of us. We must not get discouraged by how people treat us or by circumstances that don't work out as we thought they should. We must always remember that the Christian serves a sovereign God who will work everything out for their good and His glory. The Bible tells us,

How I Changed

"And we know that all things work together for good to them that love God, to them who are the called according to his purpose." Romans 8:28

After I became a Christian I married my Alexandra. I will share that part of my story later. She has played an important role in my life and walk with the Lord.

Shortly after becoming a Christian I met a young couple who became good friends. The man asked me to go in partnership with him in the landscaping business. I agreed. We began working and making money, and things were going well. Then one day my partner came to me and said he wanted to end our partnership and thought I should return to the Northeastern United Sates. This caused me to be confused. God was prospering me. I had my apartment and a good business. Now God was ending my work. I didn't know what to do.

I went home and prayed for the Lord to lead me. This happened on a Monday. I was still very confused and didn't know what God would do. I was also working at Wal-Mart. The next day, Tuesday, when I went to work I jokingly said to a friend that I was selling a few things. He agreed to look at what I had to sell. So he came to my apartment and said he would buy everything. At that moment I felt impressed to sell him everything for $700.00, which was much less than it was worth.

It seemed clear to me the Lord was leading. I called my friend who I was in business with and he told me I could have the truck we had used in the landscaping business. I thanked him. He said we could go to the auto dealer and sell the truck if I needed the money. So we went to the dealer together. I was able to quickly sell the truck for $2,000. Now I had $2,700. Once again I saw how quickly God can work in the behalf of those who choose to follow Him.

I also had a car my father had given to me. I was able to sell it for $300. So from Monday to Tuesday I received $3,000.

During this time I had married Alexandra, which I will share in more detail in another chapter titled, "A Love Story." I had my wife check with the airport to see about the cost of getting tickets to fly to New York City. I thought I would buy the tickets when we arrived at the airport. So the next day, Wednesday, we packed our bags and went to the airport.

Upon arriving the man who checked the bags at the street side came up to us and asked for our ID. He went inside with our IDs and came back with two tickets and said, "enjoy your flight." As we were walking to the departure gate I asked Alexandra if she had paid for the tickets on a credit card. She said she had not. So as we walked to the gate I once again was amazed at how God provides for His children. He had even provided two airline tickets in some unknown manner so we could fly to where He wanted us to go. Once again God worked in mysterious ways.

We arrived in New York City and took commercial transportation to my mother's house in New Haven, Connecticut. We had to live in her living room for awhile. Alexandra enrolled in college, and I began working for a local company. It seemed now we were stuck in my mother's house. We were able to buy two cars at a very reasonable price. Again the Lord worked a miracle for us to get credit to buy good running cars.

One day a brochure came in the mail advertising religious meetings nearby. Alexandra showed it to me and wanted to attend. I realized the meetings were being given by the denomination I had been baptized by. So we attended the meetings and within a few weeks my wife was also baptized. Now the Lord had led us to be united in our faith.

I began praying about our living condition in my mother's home. The Lord kept us in her house for a good reason. I was able to share my faith with her and her husband.

Within six months I was able to find an apartment. The very day we moved into our new apartment my mother told me that she wanted me to pick her up on Sabbath so she could attend church with us. About a month later she and her husband were baptized. Again the Lord was working through all these events to lead Alexandra and me to where He wanted us to be, and led my mother and her husband to join us in our faith.

Within two years Alexandra graduated and began work in her career choice. I became more active in ministry in the church. The Lord opened the way for me to begin giving my testimony of God's leading in my life. I have been amazed at how quickly the Lord can open doors in order to get us to where He wants us. Since moving to New Haven I have had the opportunity to speak to hundreds of youth and adults in the United States and other countries.

As I reflect on these events in my life now I can clearly see the Lord's leading even at the times I didn't always understand how He was carrying out His will in my life. Sometimes it seemed confusing. I have learned it is important we continue to give our life to the Lord, ask for His direction and to simply trust Him and follow His leading. I have found He can work miracles in our life.

If you find yourself going through a situation that you don't understand, don't become discouraged. Keep seeking His guidance. Don't worry about the future. God will be faithful to His promise. He will guide you and teach you in the ways you should go. The Bible tells us.

> "Trust in the LORD with all thine heart; and lean not unto thine own understanding. In all thy ways acknowledge him, and he shall direct thy paths." Proverbs 3:5, 6

CHAPTER SEVEN

My New Life in Christ

"By the grace of God I am what I am: and his grace which was bestowed upon me was not in vain; but I laboured more abundantly than they all: yet not I, but the grace of God which was with me." 1 Corinthians 15:10

How true are these words of Paul in my life. As I look back on my life and I see the abundant grace and protection of God my heart is filled with joy and thanksgiving. He has taken me from the projects of Puerto Rico, He watched over me in federal prison and in the streets, and led me to know Him and serve Him. I thank Him everyday for another day of life. It is only because of my Lord that I live to serve Him. Many of my past friends are no longer living.

I have found that the Christian walk has its challenges. Satan will use everything he can to discourage the believer. In my case there were my non-Christian acquaintances who when I made my decision to follow Christ said, "This won't last. Give Juan time and he will be back into the old life." Then there were those even in the church that questioned if my conversion was genuine.

I can understand some of their feelings because when I came to accept Christ and began attending church I still had attitude, my manner of dress didn't fit their view of a Christian and my way of expressing myself was at times not as Christian as people felt it should be. It is important that we who attend church realize that Christian growth is a process. There will be those who come to know the Lord who will bring with them some of their old ways and attitudes. It is important that Christians give them time to grow in the Lord. Habits, mannerisms, dress and way of speaking all take time to change.

I found that the critical attitude of those who have been Christians for some years can be used by Satan to bring discouragement to the new Christian. It is important that those who know the Lord express God's love and acceptance toward the new believer. Jesus never turned anyone away with His words or looks who wanted to know and follow Him.

We can certainly see this in the lives of the disciples. Jesus called James and John the "sons of thunder" because of their quick temper and readiness to fight. Thomas has been known through the centuries as the doubter. Matthew was a tax collector, which put him in a very unacceptable position. Then there was Peter who denied his Lord three times even with an oath and cursing. The Lord doesn't choose perfect individuals to follow Him. His great joy is taking such people and by His grace changes them into His own image through out their life time.

The complete change that God brings into the Christian's life doesn't happen immediately. Even after receiving the baptism of the Holy Spirit on the Day of Pentecost Peter showed some prejudice when he separated himself from the gentile believers and ate with the Jewish Christians. Paul, the great apostle, had a severe disagreement with Barnabas over whether to take Mark with them on a missionary journey.

On a previous trip Mark had returned home not being willing to endure the hardships. So Paul didn't want to take him again. Barnabas wanted to give Mark another chance. The Bible says that Paul and Barnabas parted asunder. In short, they had a heated argument and parted still having strong negative feelings toward each other. In time their relationship healed and both were used mightily to serve the Lord.

For me personally, I have had a challenge with my temper. Numerous times I have had to apologize to someone for my "big mouth;" something I said that hurt them. This happened on many occasions. Such things will happen in the new believer's life. However, God uses these occasions to teach us that we need to be more careful about what we say, and how we react to situations that upset us. Solomon understood the problem with the tongue when he wrote,

> "Death and life are in the power of the tongue ..." Proverbs 18:2

James also understood the danger of an uncontrolled tongue.

> "Even so the tongue is a little member, and boasteth great things. Behold, how great a matter a little fire kindleth! And the tongue is a fire, a world of iniquity: so is the tongue among our members, that it defileth the whole body, and setteth on fire the course of nature; and it is set on for of hell." James 3:5, 6

The tongue can be used for good or bad. I certainly know that for a fact. My tongue was used for confrontation and deceit before I became a Christian. Now I have seen the Lord use the same tongue to teach about Jesus.

The root of the problem with the tongue is our pride and insecurities. When we feel put down we react in anger because our pride has been hurt. When this happens our sinful pride is still alive and it has not been crucified with Christ. When we are dead in Christ selfish pride, ego, and everything of self has been put to death and we need not be controlled by them any longer. As a Christian the Holy Spirit also begins teaching us God's will in every area of our life including how we are to relate to others when they offend us. The fruit of the Spirit is love, joy, peace; not anger, resentment and retaliation. It is the fruit of the Spirit that the Lord will begin bringing into our life. We may at times fail in some areas. Thank the Lord that when we do we can be forgiven, and treated by God as though we had never sinned.

> "My little children, these things write I unto you, that ye sin not. And if any man sin, we have an advocate with the Father, Jesus Christ the righteous." 1 John 2:1

> "If we confess our sins, he is faithful and just to forgive us our sins, and to cleanse us from all unrighteousness." 1 John 1:9

Coming from a gang background I have had a struggle with my anger. Before becoming a Christian my anger raged many times, and whenever someone confronted me I was ready to kill and that is no exaggeration. After becoming a Christian when someone would confront me I had a struggle keeping my cool. On one occasion an individual confronted me in a cafeteria on my job and said "Get the ____________ out of my way." I had done absolutely nothing to make him angry toward me. He invited me to take it outside. I said nothing in return, but in my mind I saw me breaking his head open.

When I sat down to eat my lunch I couldn't handle it any longer. So I got up and confronted him and said, "I'll break your mouth!" He just stared at me. In that moment I knew I was doing wrong, but a force kept driving me to confront him and another force was driving me to walk away. Then I felt terrible that I had misrepresented Christ in front of other people who knew I was a Christian. I was filled with remorse and sorrow. I walked away and started crying because I had failed Jesus.

About a half hour later his friends brought him to me to apologize. They knew I was a Christian, and that he shouldn't have said what he did. When he apologized I said, "I am the one who needs to apologize." So I did with tears in my eyes. He accepted my apology and we are good friends today-I even preach to him on occasion at work.

Jesus tells us to turn the other cheek and love our enemies. This is not easy and in fact is impossible for us to do of ourselves. However, with Christ all things are possible. The Bible tells us that "we are more than conquerors" (Romans 8:37).

On another occasion a similar thing happened. I was operating my machine at work and a fellow employee was staring at me. His staring was giving me a very negative feeling. So I went to him and said, "Good morning." He said to me, "Get the ________ out of here!" I asked him, "Why are you talking to me that way?" He responded, "Do you want to take it outside?" I again felt anger because of his disrespectful attitude toward me. My heart was beating fast.

When Jesus was shown disrespect and being nailed to the cross He said, "Father, forgive them for they know not what they do" (Luke 23:34). As Christians we by God's grace need to react the same way when others show us disrespect. I thank the Lord that when this man showed me disrespect that I did not react as I had before. Instead, by God's Spirit I controlled my mouth and just walked away. The Bible tells us,

> "Whoso keepeth his mouth and his tongue keepeth his soul from troubles." Proverbs 21:23

As I walked away from the man who spoke disrespectfully to me and returned to my work area I prayed for strength not to retaliate. By God's grace I was victorious. I had depended on the Lord to manifest His patience and forgiveness through me instead of yielding to my old sinful nature, which would have retaliated in words and perhaps deeds.

On that weekend I spoke at a church. On Monday I was again in the lunchroom at work and the man who showed me disrespect was there. The Holy Spirit brought the words of Jesus to my mind.

> "And when ye stand praying, forgive, if ye have ought against any: that your Father also which is in heaven may forgive you your trespasses." Mark 11:25

Therefore, I went over to him and asked if I could speak with him. He agreed. I apologized to him saying, "If I have offended you, I am sorry." He accepted my apology. We shook hands and parted with no feelings of anger toward each other. I realized that was probably the best sermon I could ever preach to him.

As I reflected on this experience I realized that it was my pride that always tried to get in the way of my apologizing to someone in that kind of situation. The Holy Spirit will bring to our mind what we should do. However, my pride said that he should apologize to me. God's Word says we need to take the initiative to make things right between us and our brother whenever we sense there is something wrong between us and them. We have a choice to make, either yield to the Holy Spirit's prompting or yield to our pride. Satan wants us to confront evil with evil. God tells us, "Be not overcome of evil, but overcome evil with good" (Romans 12:21).

For us to continually yield to the Holy Spirit we must die to selfish pride every day. Our experience needs to be the same as Paul's when he wrote.

> "I am crucified with Christ: nevertheless I live; yet not I, but Christ liveth in me: and the life which I now live in the flesh I live by the faith of the Son of God, who loved me, and gave himself for me." Galatians 2:20

In this verse we are told that Christ lives in the Christian. This is very real and not symbolic. Jesus literally lives in the believer through the baptism of the Holy Spirit, and wants to live out His life in him. If we believe this and moment by moment yield our sinful desires such as anger, pride, impatience, etc., Jesus will manifest the fruit of the Spirit in our life, which are love, joy, peace, patience, gentleness, goodness, faith, meekness, self-control" (Galatians 5:22, 23, NIV). You see, Jesus will live out these character qualities in us so that we will have His self-control and not be controlled by our negative feelings such as anger, impatience, retaliation, etc.

Because of my experience I personally know this to be very real. The old Juan would never have turned away from someone who showed me disrespect. I would have been in his face and ready to fight. After becoming a Christian this has been one of my greatest struggles. Satan has tried again and again to cause the old Juan to control me. However, I have learned that at the cross the old Juan was crucified with Jesus, and I don't have to be controlled by my old sinful desires of anger, unforgiveness and retaliation.

This will not happen in the Christian's life unless he chooses to yield his own sinful desires letting go of them and ask Jesus to manifest His pure and holy desires. I personally believe this is one of the greatest miracles of God; to change an angry, revengeful, ready to fight gang member into a forgiving and merciful person. This is the experience Jesus described when He said,

> "Take my yoke upon you, and learn of me; for I am meek and lowly in heart: and ye shall find rest unto your souls."
> Matthew 11:29

I want to mention one important thing at this point. Until the Christian learns how to rest in Christ and stop struggling with temptation his life will be a heavy burden. He wants to become like Jesus and not yield to anger, but the more he yields to temptation the more he will face failure and at times question if he is really a Christian. At times he will conclude that he will never change and have complete victory. However, when he comes to understand and experience victory in Christ the struggle will be over and he will have learned how to let Christ live out His life in him. The Bible describes this kind of relationship with Jesus in the following verses:

"… in all these things we are more than conquerors through him [Christ] that loved us." Romans 8:37

"I can do all things through Christ which strengtheneth me." Philippians 4:13

"… Christ in you the hope of glory." Colossians 1:27

"Knowing this, that our old man is crucified with him, that the body of sin might be destroyed, that henceforth we should not serve sin." Romans 6:6

"Likewise reckon ye also yourselves to be dead indeed unto sin, but alive unto God through Jesus Christ our Lord. Let not sin therefore reign in your mortal body, that ye should obey it in the lusts thereof." Romans 6:11, 12

"Whereby are given unto us exceeding great and precious promises: that by these ye might be partakers of the divine nature, having escaped the corruption that is in the world through lust." 2 Peter 1:4

"Therefore if any man be in Christ, he is a new creature: old things are passed way; behold all things are become new." 2 Corinthians 5:17

These are wonderful promises that the Lord has given us to claim. When the Christian learns how to do that he will definitely become a "new Creature" in Christ. The old sinful things of his life will have passed away, and the new things of God will be seen in his life.

Therefore, I appeal to all that read this book. You have nothing to lose and everything to gain by accepting Christ as your Savior. He will give you victory over every sinful desire and habit. As you grow in the Lord you will find the greatest happiness you have ever known. You will see the Lord use you to do marvelous things for Him. You will find great fulfillment in your life. Whatever your problems may be the Lord has the answer. And in the end you will live forever and spend eternity with God.

Those who choose Christ are pictured as building their house on the rock, while those who do not accept Christ are said to build their house on the sand. The house is symbolic of our lives. If we choose not to accept Christ and the storms of life come we will suffer great loss (Matthew 7:24-27).

So, don't delay another moment to accept Christ. Paul tells us,

> "... behold, now is the accepted time; behold, now is the day of salvation." 2 Corinthians 6:2

I want to close this chapter with the story of a six year old boy named Robert, but his mother called him Bobsy. He was dying from a terminal disease. His mother asked him what his dream was. He told her he always wanted to be a fireman. So she called the local fire department and asked if he could spend a day with them. The fireman said we can do better than that. We can make him a fireman for a day and make him a uniform.

Then he said he had to talk with the chief. He told the chief about the problem Bobsy had. The chief said, "We can do better than that. We can make him Fire Chief for a day." His mother told Bobsy and he was very excited. When the day arrived he was given his uniform and taken with the fireman on their runs to three fires. Since Bobsy was "Chief for the day" they would tell him how they would work at putting out a fire and ask him what he thought about it. Bobsy each time said, "That sounds good to me."

The TV news heard of the story and followed the fire trucks for the day. Bobsy appeared on the two evening newscasts. His dream had come true.

After a few months the fire department received a call from Bobsy's mother. She asked if they remembered him. They said,

"Yes, of course we do." She told them that he had only a few hours left to live. She asked if they would send a fireman to the hospital room to be with Bobsy when he died. The Chief said, "We can do better than that." Instead of one fireman they brought an entire crew of firemen with a hook and ladder fire truck. They extended the ladder up and through the window of Bobsy's hospital room. One of the firemen took Bobsy in his arms and that is where Bobsy died. Before he died Bobsy said to his mother, "Mommy, I am really a fireman." She replied with tears in her eyes, "Yes, Bobsy, you really are a fireman."

If the fire department was willing to make six year old Bobsy's dream come true how much more is our heavenly Father willing to make our desires for love, happiness, joy and success come true?

"... If God be for us, who can be against us?" Romans 8:31

CHAPTER EIGHT

A Love Story

I have learned that God's word is true. The Lord promises many blessings to His children as they follow His leading. In Malachi God tells us,

> "...and see if I will not throw open the floodgates of heaven and pour out so much blessing that you will not have room enough for it." Malachi 3:10, NIV

I soon discovered in my walk with the Lord that when I was faithful to him I experienced His blessings. However, whenever I turned to follow my own ways I was walking away from the blessings He wanted me to have. God has given us thousands of promises in the Bible. Our part is to claim them by faith.

Jesus told us how to receive His blessings to meet all our needs.

> "But seek first his kingdom and his righteousness, and all these things will be given to you as well." Matthew 6:33, NIV

These blessings may not come to us immediately. God in His wisdom sometimes waits until we are ready to receive them.

I know this is true because of the way the Lord led me to find a wonderful wife to share my life with. Her name is Alexandra. I met her before I gave my life to the Lord.

I was on vacation in Puerto Rico during the sentencing of my brother's killer. I was walking in a mall and saw her. We looked at each other and continued on. I again saw her in the parking lot. I began a conversation and asked her for her phone number. She said, "No I would rather you give me your number." So I did and we went our separate ways.

About three days later Alexandra called me. We began a friendship by calling one another. We went on a date and I had such a good time that I began looking at her as more than just a friend. I realized I was falling in love with her.

Before I was a Christian whenever I met a girl, but wasn't really interested in a long term relationship I would go as far as I could with her. However, when I met Alexandra I wanted much more that just a one night stand. So I treated her with great respect and did nothing to offend her. I did not try to have a physical relationship because of my respect for her.

I want to say something important to you ladies who are reading this book. If a man is really interested in you he will show you respect, and not try to have sex with you on the first few dates. In fact, God's will is that a man and woman not have sex until they are married. He has good reasons for that command. He knows there are many negative consequences for having a sexual relationship outside of marriage.

When I returned home to Connecticut I continued to call Alexandra. Our friendship grew deeper. At that time she had a boyfriend, but the relationship had problems. She would tell me how he was cheating on her, and I would give her advice. Not being a Christian I wasn't very tactful in advising her. I said, "Dump the guy!" He had been her boyfriend for ten years so it was difficult for her to end the relationship.

Because of my strong feelings for Alexandra I decided to move to Puerto Rico to live. I had a lot of emotional problems and wasn't very stable. So, I didn't have much to offer her. I didn't have a job or much future.

She picked me up at the airport and we went on a date. It didn't take her long to figure me out. She quickly saw my instability, character flaws, and the violent guy that I was. She didn't like what she saw. So she began distancing herself from me. I felt her moving away and this hurt me very much.

One day a friend of mine visited me from Connecticut. I went on a date with Alexandra along with this friend and a couple others. When on the date she made it clear to me that she wasn't interested in any relationship other than being friends. That was very discouraging especially after moving to Puerto Rico for her. I was "kicked to the curb."

I didn't take this rejection very well. I wanted to change and thought that being with Alexandra would change my life-style. I discovered that no man or woman can change us. Only by giving our life to God can we be changed. He will give us new desires and a new purpose in life. Only as we have Christ in our life can we find true happiness, peace, joy and love.

I reacted with anger at everyone else, but not at Alexandra. This was what led to me getting shot, which I related previously. I went to a bar a few days letter after that. I started drinking and using drugs. I started staring at some young men sitting around a table in the bar. I sat over by them and then for no reason jumped on one of them and started fighting. The others then jumped me and started fighting with me. During the fight I felt someone hit me with a chair on my back. I fell to the ground and immediately got back on my feet. I posed myself to continue to fight. I then saw all but one of them step aside. The one facing me pulled up his shirt and I saw a 9 mm gun. He pulled it out.

I turned and ran. I heard the gun shots while running. I could hear the bullets flying by me. As I ran I was yelling and ran to my sister-in-law's house. I went into the house and told her I had been in a fight. I then noticed that my back was bleeding under my waist. The bullet had passed through me. I went to the shower and washed the wound. Then I went to the hospital where I was treated. From there I went to my mother's house for about a week.

Because of my foolishness I could have been killed. I thank the Lord for His protection even during a time when I was walking away from Him. God is very loving and patient with His children.

I called Alexandra and told her what had happened. She felt very badly that I had almost lost my life. We began communicating again. She asked me where my father was and suggested I go live with him and get my life together. She said that she liked me, but the life-style I was living was wrong for both of us. She gave me hope that if I was able to change there was the possibility for us to have a future together.

That caused me to call my father who lived in Florida and see if I could live with him. He agreed. He was a Christian and I began going to church with him. The Lord used this experience to put me in the path He had for me. As I began walking with Jesus my relationship with Alexandra grew. The relationship between her and her boyfriend was deteriorating while ours was improving.

I was beginning to discover that as I was faithful to the Lord He was able to bless me more and more. However, soon I began drifting away from the Lord again. I was hanging out with the wrong kind of people. We would drink and do drugs. I lost my job, lost Alexandra, and even got arrested. This is when I got my head split open. The Bible tells us.

> "There is a way that seems right to a man, but in the end it leads to death." Proverbs 14:12, NIV

I found this to be very true in my life. Whenever I began going "my own way" that seemed right to me I began getting into more and more difficulty. If I had continued on that path I would be dead today.

After suffering these losses I once more gave my life to the Lord and began walking with Him. He began blessing me. One of the greatest blessings was that the He brought Alexandra back into my life.

Alexandra and I began communicating again. She was pleased with the changes that were taking place in my life. I flew her to Florida where I was, which allowed our relationship to grow stronger. I was determined to be faithful to the Lord and not enter into an improper sexual relationship with her. This was at times a test for me. I was learning that as a Christian we still will face trials and temptations, but the Lord will give us the victory.

The Lord had brought Alexandra to me. It would have been easy for me to justify my actions when tempted to enter into an improper relationship with her. However, the Lord wants us to be faithful to Him in all situations, even when we want something very much, but we know it is not God's will for us to have it.

I also discovered that when we wait for the Lord He gives us the very best. By choosing to follow God's will in our relationship we were able to come even closer together emotionally and spiritually. Before too long we decided we wanted to spend the rest of our lives together. I asked her to marry me and she said yes. This took place about a week after she came to Florida. We had been friends for three years and we knew we wanted each other.

Alexandra had been a "hip hop" promoter in clubs in Puerto Rico. So she had been involved in music and activities that were very un-Christian. I had been praying for the Lord to take her away from that life-style. If she was the woman for me I knew she had to get away from those worldly things. The Lord tells us in the Bible,

> "For I know the plans I have for you, declares the LORD, plans to prosper you and not to harm you, plans to give you hope and a future. Then you will call upon me, … and I will listen to you." Jeremiah 29:11, 12, NIV

The Lord answered my prayers for Alexandra in an unexpected way. Her promoting business began failing. In time she lost her job. Bills began piling up and other problems came into her life. That was the time I invited her to come to Florida so we could spend some time together. The Lord had removed the obstacles in her life, which enabled her to agree to come. The Lord works in unexpected ways to answer our prayers. He will at times put us in situations that we don't understand. However, we can be sure He has a purpose in placing us there.

Sometimes we need to hit rock bottom and lose control of our life before we are open to turn to God. Alexandra had almost lost her life on a couple occasions. God brought her to the point where she was open to His leading. God had plans for her as well as me, plans for a ministry together. For this to happen we both had to go through some difficult, personally breaking times, which God used to bring us to the point to be open to His leading in our lives and say yes to following Him all the way.

The Lord put it in my heart to obey Him. The Bible says.

> "How can a young man keep his way pure? By living according to your word." Psalm 119:9, NIV

I knew the importance of following the Lord. I had lived a very ungodly life for many years and I had no real joy and peace. Now I wanted to follow God's Word and keep my way pure. I knew it was important that the woman I would marry had the same desire. The Bible says we should not be "unequally yoked" with unbelievers in marriage. God knows such a marriage would make it more difficult for the believer to follow Him.

The Lord led me to put His will above my desires when it came to my relationship with Alexandra. Therefore, my prayers concerning Alexandra involved my willingness to submit to God's will along with asking Him to bring changes in her life. I had to be willing to put my desires aside and look for God's will in my life. It is important we wait for the Lord to answer our prayer even if He delays the answer or we don't get the answer we want.

God knows what is best for us. It is important we trust Him and believe He will give us only the best even if we don't think it is the best at the time. Sometimes God is answering our prayers, but we don't want to accept it. Often we pray simply asking God to give us what we want. God loves us too much to give us something He knows is not for our good. We are His children and He is our heavenly Father.

So, Alexandra and I got married and lived in Florida for a short time and then moved to Connecticut. She attended some meetings with me where the Bible was being taught. During the meetings she accepted the Lord and decided to be baptized. Shortly after the meetings were over she was baptized and joined the church with me. Now we were completely united in our faith and both of us wanted to follow the Lord wherever He would lead.

The Lord then began opening up ministry opportunities for me. I was asked to speak to youth and give my testimony of the Lord's leading in my life. I began to see the Lord use me to lead other youth to Christ. Alexandra also began giving her testimony and the Lord blessed by leading youth to Christ through her messages also. So we found ourselves together in ministry.

I am amazed how the Lord can take two individuals such as Alexandra and me, who were both living very worldly un-Christian lives, and bring us both in a personal relationship with Himself. Then in His own unique way also bring us together and place us in a united ministry.

What the Lord has done for Alexandra and me He can also do for you. The Bible says,

> "Trust in the LORD with all your heart and lean not on your own understanding; in all your ways acknowledge him, and he will make your paths straight." Proverbs 3:5, NIV

CHAPTER NINE

A Mother's Prayers

The Bible tells us,

"The prayer of a righteous man is powerful and effective." James 5:16, NIV

I know from personal experience that this verse could also read,

"The prayer of a Christian mother is powerful and effective."

I believe this because of my mother prayed for me. She continued to pray for me when I was running with the gang in the project, when I was involved with drugs and in prison. She never gave up, but spent hours every day on her knees fasting, praying and reading her Bible. My mother had lost one son and didn't want to lose another.

Many times I would come home from the clubs and find her reading the Bible or in prayer. I had no idea she was praying for me. In my mind she was my mother and Bible reading and prayer is what mothers do.

Now when I reflect on this I realize how unappreciative I was of her. I know now that it was because of her prayers for me that the Lord saved me so many times from being killed. I know I am now a Christian because of her prayers.

For example, the same hour on the night I was shot my mother was praying for me. She had felt I was in danger during that day, and so she went to her knees and pray for my protection. The same thing happened when I was thrown to the ground and my head was split open. She was praying for me at that very time. I know this because she asked me when these things happened, and she told me those were times she had been praying.

I know beyond any question that God hears the prayers of praying mothers. I want to encourage all mothers who read my story to never give up praying for your children. God hears every one of your prayers. He will answer them in His own way and time.

The story of Hannah in the Old Testament tells how the Lord answered a mother's prayer. Hannah had no children. So she prayed persistently to the Lord for a son. The Bible records her prayer in the book of First Samuel.

> "In bitterness of soul Hannah wept much and prayed to the Lord. And she made a vow, saying, 'O Lord Almighty, if you will only look upon your servant's misery and remember me, and not forget your servant but give her a son, then I will give him to the Lord for all the days of his life ...'" 1 Samuel 1:10, 11, NIV

God heard her prayer and gave her a son. Hannah also honored her promise to the Lord and gave her son to be instructed by the high priest in the temple. Her son's name was Samuel and he became a great prophet of God.

Concerning God's answer to her prayer Hannah said,

> "I prayed for this child, and the Lord has granted me what I asked of him." 1 Samuel 1:27, NIV

God will hear and answer the prayers of faithful mothers. So, if you have a son or daughter never stop praying for them. Your prayers can be a very powerful means of enabling the Lord to work in the lives of your children.

I have discovered in my own life the power of prayer. I also have seen many answers to prayer concerning myself, my wife, and my ministry. I encourage every young person to pray. Spend time in prayer. It is the key to enabling God to work in the lives of those we pray for. Prayer releases the power of God.

Also, prayer strengthens us. If you want to be a strong Christian you must be a man or woman of prayer and spend quality time in the Bible.

Books by Pastor Dennis Smith

The Baptism of the Holy Spirit
This book presents the biblical teaching on the baptism of the Holy Spirit, the benefits of receiving this gift in fullness, and why it is necessary for the Christian to receive it.

Spirit Baptism & Evangelism
The relationship between the baptism of the Holy Spirit and witnessing for Christ is presented along with Christ's method of evangelism.

Spirit Baptism & New Wineskin Fellowship
This book gives a biblical and historical study into how the early Christians "did church", and why it is important Christians continue to experience genuine fellowship.

Spirit Baptism & Deliverance
It is God's will to deliver His children from every influence and oppression of Satan in the Christian's life spiritually, emotionally and physically. This book presents how deliverance can become a reality in the Christian's life.

Spirit Baptism & Prayer
Prayer is the most powerful force on earth. This book presents the many facets of prayer including fasting and how to pray in the Spirit.

Spirit Baptism & Christ's Glorious Return
This book presents the characteristics of those who are ready for Christ's return.

Spirit Baptism & Abiding in Christ
This book explains how the Christian is to obtain victory over every temptation and sin by allowing Christ to live out His life in and through him or her. When this is experienced one's life will never again be the same.

Spirit Baptism & Waiting on God
This book presents the biblical teaching about waiting on God for everything: prayer, guidance, service, Christ's character, and why God allows trials and difficulties to enter the Christian's life.

Spirit Baptism & the 1888 Message of Righteousness by Faith
In 1888 God brought the message of righteousness by faith to the Seventh-day Adventist Church. This book presents what that message was and why it is essential we experience righteousness by faith in Christ alone today.

Spirit Baptism & Earth's Final Events
This book unveils Satan's last-day prophetic deceptions and reveals the role the baptism of the Holy Spirit and righteousness by faith plays in preparing God's people for earth's final events.

40 Days
A devotional book designed to be used during a 40 day time period individually or as a group. Each of the 40 daily devotionals presents one aspect of the baptism of the Holy Spirit followed by study questions, and a daily prayer focus, which includes suggestions for reaching out to 5 former or non-Adventists. An excellent book for preparing for a Visitor's Sabbath and evangelistic meetings.

Transformed By the Spirit (w/Juan Cubero)
The inspiring true story of Juan Cubero, a former violent drug dealer and prison gang leader, who the Spirit transformed to become a servant of the King of kings. An amazing story for young and old alike.

Pastor Smith's books can be ordered from:
Adventist Book Center - 800-435-0008

Dennis Smith
Phone: 203-389-4784
Email: smith06515@msn.com
Website: www.spiritbaptism.org

more resources

from Transformed by the Spirit Ministry

english

DVD My Testimony CD-SERMON

CD-1 Guard Well the Avenues of the Soul **CD-2** The Death of Nadab and Abihu **CD-3** The Lost Son **CD-4** The Boy Jesus at The Temple **CD-5** The Calling of the First Disciples **CD-6** Builders of The Wall **CD-7** My Testimony

spanish

CD-SERMON 1-Protengiendo los Sentidos (Guard well the Avenues of the Soul) 2-DVD-Campaña evangelista Transformado 3-Frente Al Rio Jordan 4-Elige Tu Camino 5-Estas Perdido Busca A Jesus 6-Dicernimiento Espiritual 7-El Caracter de los Dicipulos 8-Es Hora de Marchar 9-Atrevete a Esperar 10-Restaurando Emociones

contact

Transformado.org cell: (203) 815-4914 home: (787) 657-2715
email: jaycubero@yahoo.com my space: jcuberodwtk@yahoo.com
facebook: Jaycubero@yahoo.com